STREET NAI
MILTON KEYNES
SOUTH

STREET NAMES OF MILTON KEYNES SOUTH

ANNE BAKER

Phillimore

2006

Published by
PHILLIMORE & CO. LTD
Shopwyke Manor Barn, Chichester, West Sussex, England
phillimore.co.uk

ISBN 1-86077-412-1
ISBN 13 978-1-86077-412-6

Printed and bound in Great Britain by
THE CROMWELL PRESS
Trowbridge, Wiltshire

CONTENTS

ACKNOWLEDGEMENTS

I would like to thank John Platt, former Secretary to the Board of Milton Keynes Development Corporation, for agreeing to write the Foreword to this book and, as the man originally charged with the task of naming the streets of the new city, making the project possible in the first place. Also Liz Preston, Milton Keynes City Discovery Centre; and Ruth Meardon of the Local Studies Centre, Milton Keynes Library for access to their archive. All those who provided photographs, including David Watts, Peter Hoare and the staff of the Centre for Buckinghamshire Studies; Brett Thorn, Buckinghamshire Museum; Stephen Ovens of Bletchley Park Trust, and Scott Grace. Jane Forder of Bletchley and Fenny Stratford Town Council and Bob Burt for help with Bletchley names. Not forgetting my family for their support and encouragement and, last but not least, my husband John, who wrote the Introduction to this book and helped in so many ways before he died in November 2004.

Dedication

In memory of my husband
John Anthony Baker
1935-2004

FOREWORD

There is a wealth of history in the names in Milton Keynes. They act as a daily reminder of the people who lived in the area through the ages, their way of life, their use of the land and the skills and trades they practised. Sir Frank Markham, in his introduction to the first volume of his *History of Milton Keynes and District* (1973), hoped that the new generation in Milton Keynes might 'wish to know of its past, and to retain the best of it'. Sir Frank was a great believer in the continuity of communities and the value of roots. He had been an opponent of the proposal to build a new town in North Buckinghamshire, but, faced with the decision to go ahead, he and a number of other local people sought to engage with the planners in order to have new development complement the existing settlements. They were particularly anxious to see Stony Stratford and the villages incorporated into the new city in a form they would find acceptable and to make the new city something of which they, too, could be proud. Happily for all concerned, as Michael Reed, later one of the founding Directors of the City Discovery Centre, noted in *The Buckinghamshire Landscape* (1979), the Development Corporation took 'an enlightened attitude towards conservation'.

I remember back in 1973 Sir Frank and Lady Markham walking with Fred Roche, Stuart Mosscrop and Chris Woodward, round the area of the Secklow Mound and down the quiet green lane that ran from Bradwell Common to the Great Linford-Little Woolstone road. Sir Frank, who wanted to impress on the Corporation the long history of the area and the role of the Secklow Hundred as a 'centre of government', was greatly encouraged by the willingness of the designers to listen to his enthusiastic presentation of the past. One of those on this walk was a devotee of the theory of ley lines and would later propose the 'midsummer solstice' pattern of naming for the boulevards. Sir Frank wrote to me in October 1974, a year before he died, expressing the hope 'that my work may in some way help to produce a fine civic consciousness in the great new city'. He never saw the city centre, but I am sure he would have been delighted with the naming of the boulevards and with the incorporation of the Secklow Mound behind the Library.

The names found in Milton Keynes are by no means all from the growth of the new city. Areas like Bradwell, Fenny Stratford, Loughton and Stony Stratford, to name but a few, all contain road names from long before the designation of a new city. So, it was only sensible that, from the beginning, the Development Corporation should have taken naming seriously and welcomed, in 1968, an approach from Newport Pagnell RDC on the question of preserving the history of the area when identifying elements of the new city. Bob Dunbabin, the Clerk of Newport Pagnell RDC, and Ray Bellchambers, then a member of the RDC and a Corporation Board Member, were particularly keen to see the old merged into the new. The Corporation indicated its willingness to take the initiative on naming and I (with a more than passing interest in history) was deputed to do the work. The Local Authorities Joint Liaison Committee endorsed the proposal that the Corporation should take the lead and one of our first acts was to send Sue Godber to see Mr Shirley at Peartree Farm, Woughton-on-the Green, to collect field names; Eaglestone was one of the fruits of this visit.

A small group of MKDC Board Members (Ray Bellchambers, Margaret Durbridge and Jim Cassidy), with a highways engineer (John Rowlands) and myself, devised and put forward the proposals for naming the city areas and the city's H and V roads, and the Board of the Development Corporation cleared the proposals before they were submitted to the local authorities, which had the legal responsibility for such matters. Nearly all the proposals made by the Corporation were accepted, although Wolverton UDC was not happy with the name Hodge Furze and requested a change to Hodge Lea. Those of us who liked the idea of naming the city centre Secklow were over-ruled before any proposals left the Corporation. The local authorities, particularly Newport Pagnell RDC and UDC and Wolverton UDC, played a very helpful part in the process, being keen to conserve all sensible links between the past and the new city's future. Bletchley UDC, which, in my view, was never very enthusiastic about the Development Corporation's role, was unwilling to see defined and named areas created within the UDC boundaries or to anticipate the naming and navigational needs of the wider city road system.

Naming the 'city roads' and CMK 'gates' was one opportunity to conserve long gone aspects of local history, such as Secklow (914), Snelshall Priory (12th century), the Portway (a 13th-century route to Newport), and Groveway (1781). I remember taking the name for Dansteed Way from Dansteed Furlong (Dunstead 1641), mentioned in the book *The Roman Roads of South-East England*. The archaeologists had not yet discovered an ancient settlement in the area – but there was indeed a 'place on the hill', as Dennis Mynard was later happy to tell me! If Dr Margaret Gelling had published her book *Place-Names in the Landscape* (1984) twenty years earlier, we would have been better equipped to spot more significant names from the past.

To 'name' an urban area the size of Milton Keynes was not an easy task. As the opening of new areas and the building of houses gathered pace, the co-operation of developers had to be sought. Some of them were wont to use unimaginative 'catalogue lists' of names for their schemes, which they repeated in towns all over the country. We were ably supported by the new Milton Keynes Borough Council in our efforts to broaden the developers' horizons, the Council sharing our desire to see varied and interesting names adopted. We sought to introduce 'different' themes, particularly in the early years. The Corporation broke new ground with the landscaping of Milton Keynes; we tried in our small way to bring some variety into the naming too.

Pleasing everybody is, of course, impossible, names being a matter of personal taste. It has to be borne in mind that even names low down in the order of things – such as a small residential close on the edge of Milton Keynes – have to be unique if confusion is to be avoided in postal and traffic terms. Producing around 2,000 of them between 1970 and 1992 was not easy; they all had to be cleared by the appropriate councillor as well as by the Council itself. Where did the new city's names come from? Well, many backgrounds, as Anne Baker has recorded so carefully. In the villages history was the usual basis and the Heritage Map (1983), compiled by Bob Croft and Brian Giggins, shows the background to some of the historical names used in the city. Elsewhere themes were selected from which suitable names could emerge, as at Heelands where it was decided to use names from the North-West Yorkshire Highlands, an area with which one of those responsible had a personal family link. Myrtle Bank (Stacey Bushes) reminded me of a hotel in Kingston, Jamaica. Other names were reminiscent of far-flung places known to those involved (in one case a distant holiday home). The 'rock stars' theme at Crownhill was suggested by a local resident who was a member of the Elvis Presley Fan Club, Elvis being 'the King'. Ray Bellchambers made a number of suggestions for names in the Stantonbury and Bradwell areas. The names in Campbell Park were selected in appreciation of the role of Lord Campbell of Eskan in the development of Milton Keynes. Many people made contributions to the bank of names.

Sometimes there were objections. One university-educated resident complained to Wolverton UDC that the name 'Blackdown' at Fullers Slade had unfortunate racial connotations and was unacceptable; he was apparently unaware that the theme was hills and that the Blackdown Hills are in Devon. On another occasion I was asked why such a boringly ordinary name as 'William Smith Close' was used at Woolstone; explanation of the importance of William Smith and his steam plough put that right. Milton Keynes Parish Council invited me to a meeting to explain why such unknown and irrelevant names had been put forward for their village; again, explanation of the historical context of the names was accepted by the villagers. A sign of the times was a reluctance in the early 1970s to see one name attached to a road with both rental and sale housing schemes on it – or even to see the schemes sharing the same access road! By the 1980s such views had disappeared. At Kiln Farm, where the names were in place before many occupants arrived, I received a strong reaction to the spine road being called 'Pitfield'; in this case, the names had been officially approved, but I was told in very straight terms how detrimental to marketing a name like 'Pitfield' would be. I still cannot see the problem (it was after all an old brickmaking area, hence Brickkiln Farm). No London banks seemed to find an address in 'Cheapside' a disadvantage.

One of the last naming tasks I undertook personally, together with highways engineer John Wardley, was the naming of the city road roundabouts. If anyone I meet – in places far from Milton Keynes – has been to the new city, it is the roundabouts they talk about. Despite the Corporation's Information Unit producing city road maps from 1975 and placing Information Boards (incorporating maps) in lay-bys at the entrances to the Designated Area from 1976, the H and V roads and the roundabouts have always defeated some sections of society. We discovered early in the development that lorry drivers mastered map-reading and the navigation system fairly quickly, but those with high-powered cars or higher education found them difficult!

It is hard to believe that it is nearly forty years since the new city project began and it is heartening to see a book incorporating the results of what was essentially a 'backroom' task among the complex and highly technical responsibilities of the Development Corporation. It would be remiss of me not to take the opportunity to acknowledge the contributions made by Ralph Bailey (BMK) and Teresa Jenkins and Val Sharpe (MKDC) over a long period. In addition to their real jobs, they coped with the naming of roads in a multitude of housing developments throughout the new city – a sometimes thankless task, although fascinating to look back on. I also remember well the kindness and support received in the early days from the late Colin Rees, when he was Wolverton UDC's Chief Engineer, and the co-operation received over many years from Dennis Mynard and the staff of the Archaeology Unit.

JOHN PLATT

Secretary to the Board of the
Milton Keynes Development Corporation 1983-92

INTRODUCTION
by John Baker

When in 1967 nearly forty square miles of North Buckinghamshire countryside was designated for the building of Britain's biggest New Town, it was a decision which stirred the emotions of people then living in the three towns and 13 villages in the area.

Many people, particularly those in the northern towns of Wolverton and Stony Stratford, were totally opposed to the concept. Ten miles south, however, the majority of Bletchley residents were far more welcoming, living as they did under an urban authority which had been involved in building 'overspill' accommodation, mainly for Londoners, since shortly after the end of the Second World War.

In 1962, Buckinghamshire's chief architect and planning officer, Fred Pooley, had produced proposals for a city in which the transport system would be based on a monorail with townships of up to 7,000 people built along the route and with no homes more than seven minutes' walk from a station. The object of Pooley's vision was instantly tagged 'Pooleyville' by the local press.

It has been said that Pooley's vision 'laid the foundations' for a future city, although initially it produced considerable squabbling among national, county and local politicians during the early years of the 1960s. This makes it all the more surprising to recall that, by early 1966, the concept finally came into focus in the shape of a map produced by Richard Crossman, Labour's Minister of Housing and Local Government at that time. It revealed an area (later reduced after a public inquiry to 21,900 acres, roughly 34 square miles) on which it was planned to build the biggest New Town of them all, with a population of a quarter of a million people.

Suddenly, speed was of the essence.

Within a matter of months, the Draft North Buckinghamshire New Town (Designation Order) was made and announced by Anthony Greenwood, who had succeeded Crossman. The name Milton Keynes was chosen from one of the villages in the area – a choice strongly supported by Lord Campbell of Eskan, the first appointed Chairman of Milton Keynes Development Corporation, as acknowledging the hybrid of the poet Milton and the internationally acclaimed economist, John Maynard Keynes.

With the appointment of the Main Consultants, Llewelyn-Davies Weeks Forestier-Walker and Bor, and members of the Board of the Corporation, concentration was focused on establishing the key issues affecting the widest range of planning and social objectives, the goals of architects and engineers, the search for vital decisions over the vexed question of the city's transport system, projected housing densities and the siting and size of the new main shopping centre.

Problems on a scale never before encountered were overcome, one by one, as a direct result of the involvement of many of the country's finest planners, architects and engineers gathered together by a Corporation determined to meet the challenges and opportunities presented to make the venture the success it has undoubtedly become.

The Plan for Milton Keynes, which followed an Interim Report a year earlier, was produced for limited distribution among Board members and senior officers late in 1969. Its two volumes were formally launched at a press conference the following March and a Public Inquiry, lasting ten days, took place towards the end of June.

Opposition to the Plan had by now largely dissipated as work began on putting in the first phases of the city's infrastructure. The grid road system as we know it today, started with a section of the H2 (Millers Way) east of the V7 (Saxon Street), there were presentations of plans for specific areas, the first MKDC housing schemes got underway at Simpson and in Stony Stratford, the Open University arrived at Walton Hall, and proposals for the central area of Bletchley and for the two northern towns were presented.

It was all systems go. Then came the shock announcement that the little village of Cublington, near Wing, had been listed among the possible sites for the third London airport. The impact of this news sent shockwaves through most people living in North Buckinghamshire. A poll conducted by the *Milton Keynes Gazette* revealed that more than 90 per cent opposed the plan, which would also have the effect of turning Milton Keynes into an airport city.

The Hon. Mr Justice Roskill, chairing the Commission of Inquiry into the siting of the airport, published plans which would lead to the expansion of Milton Keynes westwards from Bletchley, through Winslow, to provide for a population of more than 400,000 people.

Lord Campbell, who was to earn the soubriquet of 'the father of Milton Keynes', led the fight, strongly supported by press and public, against the proposal which became, for him, a resignation issue. In evidence to the Commission, he went as far as to suggest that grafting an airport onto that part of Milton Keynes which would have been developed by 1987, 'could only produce a mongrel city'. He was subsequently joined in opposition by Professor Colin Buchanan, an architect and town planner who was also a Commission member. His dissenting report ultimately saved the city as we know it today.

Cublington was dropped by the government from the list of possible sites in April 1971 and over the past two decades the plan has become reality.

Development on this scale could only have come about as a result of the participants' belief in the Plan and their collective and individual belief in their abilities, led by a man who was a passionate believer in Milton Keynes.

THE GRID ROADS

The main thoroughfares through Milton Keynes are designed in the pattern of a grid, each square enclosing an estate. The grid roads are numbered vertically – V 1-11 called Streets, and horizontally – H 1-10 called Ways. Even before Roman times, there were several ancient trackways crossing the area which is now Milton Keynes, particularly from west to east, and most of the H Ways have taken their names.

Snelshall Street (V 1)   Refers to Snelshall Priory which stood about a mile and a half to the south-west of nearby Whaddon church. The priory was founded in about 1219 and stood in 11 acres of surrounding countryside.

Tattenhoe Street (V 2)   Named after the tiny village of Tattenhoe, now incorporated in the Tattenhoe area of Milton Keynes. The site of the Norman homestead of Tattenhoe has been preserved.

Fulmer Street (V 3)   Meaning 'the foul mere', Fulmer takes its name from an ancient pond at Shenley Brook End. Also, Fulmoor Close is marked on a 1771 Plan and Survey of Shenley as a field owned by William Brice.

Watling Street (V 4)   This is the section of the old Roman road between Fenny Stratford and Stony Stratford. Until the arrival of Milton Keynes, it was a stretch of the A5 until a new section of the A5 was constructed in the 1970s so that through traffic could have an uninterrupted passage through the new city. The name Watling Street derives from the ninth-century *Waeclinga straet,* meaning 'a Roman road identified with the followers of a man called Wacol', believed to have been centred around St Albans, an early name for which was *Waeclingaceaster.*

Great Monks Street (V 5)   Passes by Bradwell Abbey following the route of an old track along which the monks once traversed.

Grafton Street (V 6)   In the 18th century the Dukes of Grafton (family name Fitzroy) held substantial lands and property in south Northamptonshire, owning several local villages including Deanshanger and Paulerspury. They had a great mansion, Wakefield Lodge, near Potterspury, about a mile from Stony Stratford, where, according to Frank Markham in his *History of Milton Keynes and District*, the Graftons did most of their shopping and tipped the tradesmen with braces of pheasant or partridge. Descended from Charles II, the 3rd Duke was Prime Minister 1768-9 and the 4th Duke (1821-1918) was a well-known local figure.

Saxon Street (V 7)   This street leads to and passes through the centre of Milton Keynes, which is built at the highest point in the area and on the site of Secklow Corner, the ancient Saxon meeting place of the Secklow Hundred.

Marlborough Street (V 8)   The Dukes of Marlborough were associated with the Milton Keynes area after Sarah, Duchess of Marlborough purchased the Stantonbury estates in 1727. She gave it to her grandson, John Spencer, and the lands remained in the ownership of the Earls Spencer of Althorp, Northamptonshire until well into the 19th century. Marlborough Street begins at Stantonbury and skirts the east side of the modern estate.

Overstreet (V 9)   Following the line of a 17th-century track near Downs Barn, this is a short stretch of carriageway connecting Campbell Park with Great Linford. The affix *Over* usually indicates a place 'at the ridge or slope'.

Brickhill Street (V 10)   Named after the villages of Little, Great and Bow Brickhill from where this street begins on its journey northwards to meet the Wolverton road at Great Linford. It replaces an ancient road which ran beside the river Ouzel to Danesborough, an historic hill fort in the woods above Bow Brickhill. According to the *Oxford Dictionary of English Place Names,* Brickhill has nothing to do with bricks, but derives from the Celtic *brig* meaning 'hill top' and the Old English *hyll.*

Tongwell Street (V 11)   Named after the field on which stood Tongwell Farm, shown on an 1806 map of Newport Pagnell. Tongwell Street runs from Old Farm Park to the outskirts of Newport Pagnell.

Ridgeway (H 1)   This is a short section of the prehistoric Ridgeway track which ran from Avebury on Salisbury Plain to the east coast at the Wash.

Millers Way (H 2)   This was the first of the new city roads to be built. It follows the line of an old track which ran between Bradwell windmill and Stony Stratford, hence the name Millers Way.

Monks Way (H 3)   Skirting the site of Bradwell Abbey, this name refers to the monks which once inhabited the abbey and traversed the tracks and pathways in the area.

Dansteed Way (H 4)   Danstead was an ancient site and field name, 'Long Danstead and Short Danstead', shown on a 1678 plan of the area. It is tempting to suggest that the site may have been a homestead occupied by the Danes, but excavations carried out in 1979-81 revealed it to be the site of an Iron-Age/Saxon village. There were, however, many savage raids by the Danes in the early 1000s AD, including an invasion of Newport Pagnell, and several Danish settlements in the area now covered by Milton Keynes. The road runs from Grange Farm in the west to Newport Pagnell.

Portway (H 5)   A Roman route running from Whaddon, through Shenley and Seckloe, to Willen was known by AD 1250 as 'Rector's Portway', and 'Dichefurlong by Portwei'. The new thoroughfare which has taken its name follows close to the old track. Port, meaning a town, or market town, identifies this as 'the way to town' i.e. Newport Pagnell.

Childs Way (H 6)   This takes its name from an 18th-century track and field name in east Loughton, by which the road passes on its way from Shenley Common Farm in the east to the M1 at junction 14. An archaic meaning of child (or childe) was a young nobleman. Alternatively, someone named Child(s) may have owned or farmed land in Loughton.

Chaffron Way (H 7)   This was the name of an 18th-century track through Woughton, by which the modern Chaffron Way passes. A chaffron, or chamfron, is a piece of leather or plate of steel worn by a horse to protect its face in battle. The reason for its use here is obscure.

Standing Way (H 8)   This follows the route of an ancient track which, it is believed, linked Buckingham, via Thornborough, to Watling Street and the Roman station of Magiovinium near Fenny Stratford. Today it is the A421, which runs from Buckingham to the A1, east of Bedford. The name Standing may be a derivation of the Old English word *staning* meaning 'stony places'.

Groveway (H 9)   Groveway has been in existence and called by this name since at least the 18th century. It travels from Watling Street at Bletchley to the north side of Wavendon, where it gives way to the ancient London road, coming in from Hockliffe, through Woburn and on to Newport Pagnell. Presumably it once passed through the groves of walnut and other trees which grew in this area.

Bletcham Way (H 10)   This was the name of another 18th-century track which passed through Woughton. The name derives from *Blecca's-ham*, the Old English meaning 'homestead of a man called Blecca'. The present road runs from Bletchley to Wavendon Gate.

A Note on OS Map References

The Ordnance Survey (OS) numbers referred to are taken from the Milton Keynes Development Corporation's paper *Names in Milton Keynes* (1992) and are from a 1:2500 scale edition updated in 1965. A collection of old maps may be seen, by appointment, at Milton Keynes City Discovery Centre, Bradwell Abbey, or at the Local Studies Centre, Central Milton Keynes Library.

SIMPSON

GRANBY   MOUNT FARM   TILBROOK

CALDECOTTE

DENBIGH

WEST
BLETCHLEY

OLD BLETCHLEY   FENNY
STRATFORD
CENTRAL
BLETCHLEY

FAR BLETCHLEY

BLETCHLEY

WATER EATON

THE LAKES
ESTATE

BLETCHLEY

Bletchley, known in the 12th century as Blechelai, or Blaecca's-lea, meaning 'woodland clearing of a man called Blaecca', started life as an agricultural settlement, with a church first built there around 1190. After the Norman Conquest, two manors were established, known as Church Bletchley and West Bletchley, both under the lordship of the de Grey family. The oldest surviving relic of Bletchley's distant past is Rectory Cottages, originally built in 1447 and moved to its present site in 1618. It has an unusual medieval hammerbeam roof. Bletchley remained little more than a village until the coming of the railways in the 19th century caused expansion and put it on the map as a 'railway town'. With the urgent need for housing after the Second World War, the town expanded further, and yet again with the arrival of Milton Keynes. Bletchley is divided into nine separately named areas and some of the connecting road names tend to overlap.

CENTRAL BLETCHLEY

THEME Parish History

Albert Street   Named after Albert, the Prince Consort and husband of Queen Victoria.

Ashfield Grove   Probably built on a field where ash trees grew, although another local connection was Edmund Ashfield who, in 1563, was granted the manor of Shenley and also the site of Snelshall Priory, which was close to Whaddon.

Barons Close   On the theme of royal titles given to roads north of the town centre, a baron is the lowest rank of British nobility. Originally, during the Middle Ages, a baron was any tenant-in-chief of a king or other overlord.

Bedford Street   This refers to the town of Bedford, the next station on the Oxford to Cambridge railway line which runs through Bletchley. Also, the Bedford Railway Company was involved in the building and running of the railway which was opened on 17 November 1846 to the sound of church bells and the Bedford Brass Band playing.

Birchfield Grove   Probably built on a field where birch trees grew.

Brooklands Road   This road was developed on the land once attached to the 17th-/18th-century Brooklands Farm, which lay close to Eaton Brook, which flows westward into the river Ouzel at Water Eaton.

Browne Willis Close   Named after the renowned antiquarian and local benefactor, Browne Willis, who was lord of the manors of Bletchley, Fenny Stratford and Water Eaton during the 18th century. He built St Martin's church, Fenny Stratford and spent much of his money on restoring other local churches, including St Mary's, Bletchley. He lived at Whaddon Hall but, in 1710, built in Bletchley Park a tall mansion which he called Water Hall after the demolished mansion at Water Eaton. He made little use of it and it was pulled down after his death in 1760.

Sign on the Brunel Shopping Centre, Bletchley.

Brunel Centre   This covered shopping arcade was built in the 1960s and named in honour of Isambard Kingdom Brunel (1806-59), the engineer famed for his ships and bridges such as the *Great Eastern* and Clifton Suspension Bridge, to name but two of his many great works.

Cambridge Street   Recalls the Cambridge to Oxford railway line which ran through Bletchley.

Cawkwell Way   Named after Mr W. Cawkwell, a railway manager who was elected as Chairman of the London & North Western Railway Company Special Committee in the 19th century.

Chandos Place   The Marquess of Chandos was Chairman of the London & North Western Railway (LNWR) from 1853 to 1861 when, on the death of his father, he inherited the title Duke of Buckingham. He remained fervently involved with the building of the new railway line and did much to improve the family seat at Stowe.

Clifford Avenue   Takes the name of a 1950s Bletchley councillor, Clifford Flack.

Dukes Drive   A duke is a nobleman of high rank, and usually owner of a large estate, such as the Duke of Bedford.

Duncombe Street   The Duncombe family have held the manor of Great Brickhill since 1527 and still live there today. By the 1600s they had bought the manor of Broughton and in the late 18th century purchased 700 acres of Bletchley, expanding further in the 1870s when they owned the whole of Water Eaton, making them one of the largest landowners in the Milton

Duncombe Street, Bletchley in the 1970s.

Keynes area. During the mid-19th century, Philip Duncombe became a close friend and advisor to Benjamin Disraeli, who became MP for North Bucks, and Prime Minister, and often stayed at Great Brickhill Manor.

Earls Close   An earl is a nobleman ranking below a marquess and above a viscount.

Eaton Avenue   This avenue divides Central Bletchley from the Water Eaton area of the town.

Findlay Way   George Findlay was General Manager of the London & North Western Railway Company in the 19th century. Coincidentally, a Findlays tobacconist shop once stood on the corner of this road.

Knowles Green   Knowles Piece and Knowles Green End are identified as fields on 18th-century maps. The land belonged to the Knowles family, who also owned the site of the Old Bletchley Road school. This was later purchased by the Leon family, who built the original Leon Secondary school on the site. The school then moved to new buildings on Drayton Road, taking the Leon name with it. The old school buildings became a nursery, first and middle schools and adopted the name of Knowles.

Lennox Road   Said to be named after the Earl of Lennox. In 1603, after the death of Elizabeth I, Thomas, Lord Grey de Wilton, lord of the manors of Eaton and Bletchley, was involved in a plot to put Arabella Stuart, daughter of the Earl of Lennox, on the English throne in place of James I. The plot failed and, in order to secure a favourable welcome at the Court of James I, Arabella betrayed details of the plot to the King, who ordered the arrest and execution of Lord Grey and his accomplices, Lord Cobham and Sir Griffin Markham.

Leon Avenue   In the 19th century, Sir Herbert Samuel Leon of Bletchley Park was a local benefactor and, with about a square mile of property, was the second largest landowner in the area. He was a London financier, head of the Stock Exchange firm of Leon Brothers, Director of Anglo-American Telegraph Company and part-proprietor of the *Daily News*. He made a fortune and purchased the country estate of Bletchley Park in 1883. He was Member of Parliament for Buckingham from 1891-5.

Sir Herbert Leon, who built and lived at Bletchley Park.

Locke Road   Joseph Locke (1805-60) was a pupil of George Stephenson and acted as his assistant and surveyor before breaking away and becoming a civil engineer and railway builder in his own right.

Lords Close   A lord was once a feudal superior and owner of a manor. Now it is either the inherited title of a nobleman, such as an earl, baron or viscount, or a courtesy title given to the younger sons of a duke or marquess. Members of the House of Lords who are not peers of the realm are known as Temporal Lords.

Mikern Close   This is a combination of the names of Mike and Ernie French, the builders of this close.

North Gate   A small cul-de-sac off North Street.

North Street   This road heads north from the town centre but, together with Western Road, may refer to the London & North Western Railway which passed through the parish in the 19th century.

Oliver Road   Said to have been named after Oliver Wells, a 1950s Bletchley councillor who is described by Sir Frank Markham in his *History of Milton Keynes and District* as 'an outspoken socialist cobbler'. He began his working life on the railways as an engine cleaner, but after losing both legs in a railway accident in 1899, he took up cobbling. However, with his two brothers, Allen and Costa, most of his life remained steeped in the railways. The Wells brothers led campaigns for social justice for railwaymen and to establish a local branch of the Labour party. After a rough ride through clashes and strikes, the National Union of Railwaymen was born in March 1912, with Oliver Wells as secretary of its Bletchley branch. In 1917 he was made a JP and a constituency Labour party was established, with Allen Wells as its organising secretary. Another Oliver of the same period was the Reverend H.F. Oliver, vicar of St Mary's parish church, Bletchley. Also a forthright crusader, he held a peace demonstration against the war in South Africa in 1900. He also objected to teetotal restrictions which Fenny Stratford UDC was trying to impose on public events and celebrations held in the town.

Osborne Street   Named after Osborne House, the royal residence on the Isle of Wight, bought by Queen Victoria and Prince Albert in 1845. It was one of Victoria's favourite homes and where she went to grieve after Albert's death. She died there in 1901.

Oxford Street   Refers to the Oxbridge railway line, running from Oxford to Cambridge through Bletchley and Bedford. Also to the Bletchley & Oxford Railway Company of which Sir Harry Verney was Chairman.

Princes Way   A fairly recent bypass of the town centre, and veering off Queensway, this sets the theme of royal titles on the small residential development leading off it.

Queensway   Originally called Bletchley Road when it passed through what is now the town centre on its way to the old village of Bletchley, it was renamed as part of an expansion scheme in the early 1950s and commemorates the accession to the throne of Queen Elizabeth II in 1952.

Regent Street   As in London, this Regent Street is conjoined to Oxford Street and is named after the Prince Regent, later George IV. As Regent, he deputised for his father, George III, who became incapable owing to insanity.

The bandstand, Queensway.

St Martins Street   St Martin became a significant saint for Browne Willis after his grandfather died on St Martin's Day in St Martin-in-the-Fields. Thus he chose St Martin as the patron saint of his church in Fenny Stratford. There is also a St Martin's Methodist Church, built 1866, in Queensway.

Sandringham Place   Queen Victoria bought the Sandringham estate in Norfolk for the Prince of Wales (later Edward VII) in 1861. A royal residence ever since, Sandringham House is where George VI was born and died and is a favourite home of his daughter, Queen Elizabeth II.

South Terrace   This is a terrace of houses to the south of the town.

Stanier Square   Sir William Arthur Stanier (1876-1965) was a railway engineer who first worked on the Great Western Railway at Swindon, becoming works manager in 1920. He was appointed Chief Mechanical Engineer of London Midland & Scottish Railway in 1932 and, between then and 1947, designed and developed numerous locomotives which bear his name, such as the 'Stanier Black Five' and the 'Stanier Tank', which ran on the Oxbridge line in the 1930s. In 1943, Stanier became scientific adviser to the Ministry of Production. He was knighted in 1944.

Stephenson House, Bletchley. Originally an office block, it is currently undergoing refurbishment into residential accommodation above 6,620 square feet of retail space.

Stephenson House   This office block was built in the 1970s near the railway station and is named after Robert Stephenson (1803-59), railway engineer, who was engineer-in-chief of the London & Birmingham Railway Company and responsible for laying the original London to Birmingham railway line in the 1830s.

Sunset Close   Close to 'the Roses' development off Water Eaton Road, this refers to the Alpine Sunset, a large-bloomed tea-rose of a peachy pink colour with a strong fragrance.

Tavistock Street   This road links Fenny Stratford and Central Bletchley. The dukes of Bedford held estates in Tavistock, Devon, giving rise to the title Marquess of Tavistock which is generally accorded to the first son of the Duke. Bedford Estates owned much of the land and property in and around Bletchley and Fenny Stratford, particularly on the south side.

The Crescent   The road forms the shape of a crescent.

Viscount Way   On the royal titles theme, a viscount is next in rank below an earl. The title was first granted in 1440 and is usually applied to the son or younger brother of a count.

Western Road   Running westerly from Fenny Stratford, as with North Street it may refer to the London & North Western Railway.

Bletchley Leisure Centre – the pyramid covers the swimming pool.

Westfield Road   The Westfield estate was built here on the field once known as West Leys.

Wetherburn Court   It is said that the first locomotive on the London to Birmingham railway line was driven by an engine driver named Wetherburn.

Windsor Street   Named after Windsor Castle in Berkshire. Originally built by William the Conqueror, it has been a royal residence ever since, with rebuildings and additions by monarchs over the centuries.

BLEAK HALL

This takes the name of Bleak Hall Farm, which lay adjacent to Peartree Lane. In the past this area was wild, uncultivated terrain and, being exposed to the east winds in particular, was recognised as somewhat bleak. There was once a cottage nearby called Starve Hall. Now there is a council depot, a household waste site, a skills centre and several companies, mostly allied to the construction industry.

THEME *Bleak House* by Charles Dickens

Chesney Wold   Chesney Wold is the name of a country house in *Bleak House* and typical of the homes lived in by the aristocracy of the 1850s. Set in Lincolnshire and surrounded by parkland, it is the country seat of Sir Leicester and Lady Deadlock and, according to the novel, it is always raining.

Summerson Road   Esther Summerson, a supposed orphan, is one
of Dickens's saintly characters who narrates part of the story. She
accompanies the main female character, Ada, when she goes to live with
John Jarndyce, another protagonist.

DENBIGH

*The area known as Denbigh was established as an industrialised area
to the east of Bletchley in the 1950s and takes the name of a notorious
18th-century inn called* Denbigh Hall. *It stood on wasteland with a
gibbet nearby, and after a murderer called Bunch was hanged there the
spot became known as Bunch Hill. In 1741 a man and a seven-year-old
boy were found murdered in a hut near Denbigh Hall and in 1805 a
shoemaker from Simpson was found robbed and murdered there. In the
1830s Denbigh Hall (also known as the* Marquis of Granby) *was used
as a labour camp for workers building the new railway. By the 1960s
the public house had become so squalid that it was demolished. North
Denbigh, which was an open space with a sports ground, is now the site
of the new Milton Keynes Dons football stadium complex.*

Bilton Road   In Denbigh East, this is named after Percy Bilton, who founded
one of the largest construction companies in the United Kingdom and in
1962 established the Percy Bilton Charity Ltd, a trust fund for the relief of
poverty, the advancement of education and other charitable purposes in the
community. Most of the firms here are connected with the auto industry.

Bond Avenue   Beginning in Denbigh East, Bond Avenue crosses Bletcham
Way and continues through Mount Farm via an old route which led to
Newport Pagnell. (See Mount Farm for name definition.)

Dane Road   The Danes unleashed a vicious assault upon north
Buckinghamshire in 830. The Danelaw boundaries included Watling Street
down to Stony Stratford and the Danes had a settlement at Simpson.

First, Second and Third Avenues   American-style street naming has been
adopted for these. A variety of engineering companies operate here.

Holdom Avenue   The Holdom family of Bletchley and Little Brickhill
produced several local councillors, beginning with Robert Holdom in 1850
and continuing through descendants to the 1970s. In 1851, Robert Holdom
with his sons George and Edward established a brewery at Fenny Stratford
which supplied most of the local pubs and villages as far out as Winslow,
Hockliffe and Deanshanger. He was also a wine and spirit merchant and
landlord of the *Bull and Butcher* in Aylesbury Street, Fenny Stratford
and the *Wellington* public house in London Road. He built the *Park Hotel*

in 1869 and in the 1870s opened a brickyard beside the railway line in Duncombe Street, Bletchley. Edward Holdom sold the brewery with all its property to Bletchley Breweries in 1896 for £14,550.

Horwood Court   The villages of Great and Little Horwood are suggested here, but the reason for the choice of name is obscure.

James Way   The name 'James' is possibly connected with one of the companies operating here. The most likely candidate is James (Jim) Marshall of Marshall Amplifications plc.

Lyon Road   This takes the name of the Lyon Automotive company which occupied a site at the head of this road until moving to other premises in Bletchley.

Romar Court   Takes the name of the Romar Service Centre which operates from a site here.

Sinclair Court   Named after Sir Clive Sinclair, British inventor of the Microvision first pocket television in 1966 and the first programmable electronic calculators, computers and numerous other electronic devices in the 1970s and 1980s. There are many electronics companies operating in Milton Keynes.

Victory Court   The reason for this choice of name is unknown.

ELFIELD PARK

Beside Watling Street and close to the National Bowl open-air theatre, this is an area of parkland set aside for motorcycle trials and other noisy sports. A new greyhound racing track and stadium is under construction to replace the old Grove Way track at Ashland which was closed in early 2006.

The area is named after Elfield Common and Elfield Close which were the names of fields shown on a 1769 map of Loughton, Ordnance Survey nos 2, 3, 4 and 24. The name is possibly a derivation of the Anglo-Saxon *hela,* meaning a heel of the parish.

FAR BLETCHLEY

THE CASTLES ESTATE

Arundel Grove   Arundel castle in West Sussex is still the home of the dukes of Norfolk. Dating from the Norman Conquest, it incorporates the many changes made over its thousand-year history. It was badly damaged during the Civil Wars, but later restored by the 8th, 11th and 15th Dukes. Its many treasures include the personal possessions of Mary Queen of Scots and items from the Duke of Norfolk's collection. The Norfolk dukedom was created in 1483 when Richard III conferred it on his friend, Sir John Howard, and the Howard name has descended to this day, carrying with it the hereditary office of Earl Marshal of England.

Bramber Close   The village of Bramber in West Sussex was once a provincial capital and port of William the Conqueror. Today the remains of the Norman castle gatehouse, walls and earthworks stand in a captivating setting overlooking the Adur valley.

Caernarvon Crescent   Caernarvon castle was the most expensive of Edward I's Welsh fortresses and took nearly fifty years to build. Begun in 1283, it takes the form of two baileys joined to create a figure-of-eight and incorporates the city walls. Having survived intact, it was the scene of the Investiture of Prince Charles as Prince of Wales in 1969 and is a World Heritage site.

Camber Close   Camber castle near Rye in East Sussex is a fine example of the many fortresses which Henry VIII built along the coast to repel possible invaders. Its purpose was entirely military and it consists of a large central keep surrounded by impregnable walls with small, round towers. The sea, which once lapped its walls, has long since receded, leaving it high and dry on the marshlands.

Chester Close   Chester is an ancient walled city where the Romans established their major camp of Deva in AD 79. In the 11th century the Normans built a motte and bailey castle on the site of the old Roman fort, and later it became the strategic base from which North Wales was attacked and conquered. Much of the castle, except for the chapel, gaol and customs house, was destroyed by Cromwell, but in 1696, after the Restoration, it was used as a mint which was managed by Isaac Newton and Edmund Halley. In a redevelopment scheme in 1788, most of the old castle was demolished and in its place rose the present building which was designed by Thomas Harrison. It is now in the care of English Heritage.

Conway Crescent and Conway Close   In North Wales, Conway castle, along with the town walls, was built by Edward I at a cost of £15,000. Its massive walls and several towers, which include the Prison tower, the King's tower, Bakehouse, Kitchen and Chapel towers, took over four years to build using the local rock and stone.

Corfe Crescent   The ruins of Corfe castle near Wareham in Dorset are a much photographed landmark. Perched strategically on top of a high tor, it was a Norman fortress commanding the way to the Purbeck Hills. During the Civil Wars, it was besieged by Cromwell and, left to decay, its stones were used in local buildings.

Dover Gate   On the Kent coast, Dover castle guarded the gateway to England from the time when it was built by the Normans until after the Second World War. Even earlier, a Roman lighthouse stood on the spot, doing the same job. It has an imposing medieval keep and battlements, an inner bailey of Henry II and 13th-century underground fortifications. Today it contains exhibitions on 'Life Under Siege' from 1216 to the Second World War and the Battle of Britain.

Harlech Place   Another of Edward I's Welsh castles, Harlech stands on a lofty rock overlooking Tremadog Bay. Edward's 'iron ring' of castles was built to subdue the Welsh and deter them from challenging English sovereignty and to repel invaders. The architect of Harlech was Master of the King's Works in Wales, James of St George, a great military engineer of his day. It is now a World Heritage site.

Kenilworth Drive   In Warwickshire, Kenilworth castle is the largest ruined castle in England, once the stronghold of kings and lords. The Earl of Leicester built a new wing especially for Elizabeth I when she came to stay for 19 days. The Great Hall still stands and the Tudor garden has been recreated.

Knarsborough Court   The ruins of 14th-century Knaresborough castle stand above the town of Knaresborough in North Yorkshire. It has a dungeon with prisoners' writings etched in the walls and an escape tunnel. It is now owned by the Duchy of Lancaster.

Lancaster Gate   An imposing medieval castle with a Norman keep, this castle dominates the city of Lancaster. It was enlarged by John of Gaunt, Duke of Lancaster and fortifications were added by Elizabeth I. It was a Parliamentary stronghold during the Civil Wars and, since the 18th century, has been used as a court house and a gaol.

Ludlow Close   Ludlow castle in Shropshire is today owned by the Earl of Powis and the Trustees of the Powis Estate. This 900-year-old castle of the Marches dates from 1086. It has been extended over the ages and became a fortified royal palace. With the establishment of the Council of Wales and the Marches, it became a seat of government. Owned by the earls of Powis since 1811, the proud edifice stands in the centre of Ludlow.

Pevensey Close   Pevensey castle in Sussex was where William the Conqueror landed in 1066 and established his first stronghold in England. Originally built between AD 250-300 as a Roman fort, it stood on the seashore and was accessible by boat. The sea has since receded and the castle stands two miles inland. Extended and garrisoned over the centuries, its substantial ruins cover a 10-acre site.

Porchester Close   Portchester castle near Portsmouth is now owned by English Heritage. It was the rallying point for Henry V's expedition to Agincourt. With a history spanning 2,000 years, it contains the most complete Roman walls in Europe.

Scotney Gardens   Scotney castle at Lamberhurst in Kent is a 14th-century moated castle. Now in ruins, with roses and clematis rambling all over it, Scotney stands like a scene from *The Sleeping Beauty* in a garden of azaleas and rhododendrons. A new Scotney castle was built in the grounds in the 1830s with a garden designed by Edward Hussey.

Warwick Road   A thousand years old, Warwick castle has a turbulent history, having witnessed murder, mystery, scandals and intrigues. There is a torture chamber in the dungeons and a ghost tower, said to be haunted by the spirit of Sir Fulke Greville, who was murdered by a manservant. The castle's history is brought to life by re-enactments for today's visitors.

GOLF COURSE ESTATE

Ainsdale Close   The Southport and Ainsdale Golf Club on Merseyside has a membership of 815. The 18-hole par 72 course was designed by James Braid and is 6,603 yards long.

Ashburnham Close   The 18-hole par 72 course of Ashburnham Golf Club at Bury Port, Dyfed in Wales has been host to the Welsh Amateur Championships and has a reputation as 'a beast of a course'. Founded in 1894 and extended from nine to 18 holes in 1902, it is a traditional links course, 6,936 yards long.

Ashridge Close   Ashridge Golf Club and course is set in beautiful parkland near Little Gaddesden, Hertfordshire. The 18-hole, par 72, 6,505-yard course was designed by Sir G. Campbell and C. and N. Hutchinson in 1932 and today the club has about 720 members. In the late 1930s, Henry Cotton (later Sir Henry) was appointed resident Club Professional, and for 12 years from 1964 broadcaster Alex Hay was the resident pro.

Birkdale Close   Royal Birkdale near Southport, Merseyside is an 18-hole golf course of 6,726 yards and par 72. It was founded in 1889 by nine gentlemen who opened a nine-hole course on a site in Shaw Hills and then moved to Birkdale Hills in 1897, where an 18-hole course was built. Unusually for the time, ladies were admitted from the beginning and one of the first tournaments held was the Ladies British Open Matchplay Championship, which was won by Dorothy Iona Campbell.

Carnoustie Grove   One of the oldest golf courses in the world, Carnoustie Championship Course was founded in 1842 and has been played over by all the golfing greats. Carnoustie Ladies Golf Club followed in 1873 and Carnoustie Hotel Golf Resort opened in 1999 in time for the Open Championship. It lies 10 miles to the east of Dundee.

Denham Close   Denham Golf Club in Buckinghamshire has a membership of around 790 and an 18-hole par 70 course, 6,456 yards long. The club was formed in 1910 by seven local gentlemen, the course opening for play in 1911. The architect was H.S. Colt, who was the first secretary of

Sunningdale Golf Club. Denham club house was originally a 16th-century farmhouse and tithe barn.

Dunbar Close   Dunbar golf course in East Lothian, Scotland is laid out on the site where Cromwell's army camped before the battle of Dunbar in 1650. Founded in 1856, the course is part of the Duke of Roxburgh's estate. Originally with 15 holes and designed by 'Old Tom Morris' (1821-1908), three more holes were added in 1880. Morris played in challenge matches and was the great golf architect of his day. He charged £1 a day, plus expenses.

Formby Close   A traditional links course close to the shoreline of the Irish Sea near Southport, Formby golf course and club was founded in 1884 by a group of 24 businessmen. It was originally nine holes, on land rented from a farmer at £10 per season. The club house was burned down in 1899 and, in about 1912, the whole course was redesigned by Willie Park and extended to 18 holes. Since then, major changes have extended the course to 6,993 yards.

Ganton Close   Eleven miles south-west of Scarborough, North Yorkshire, Ganton Golf Club has a membership of around 500. The course is 18-hole, par 73 and 6,734 yards long.

Gleneagles Close   In Perthshire, Gleneagles is home to the famous King's Course and Queen's Course which were designed by James Braid. His plan for King's Course, which opened in 1919, was to test the skills of the most accomplished golfers and Gleneagles has hosted many championship and other tournaments. The new Monarch's PGA Centenary Course, designed by the great Jack Nicklaus, opened in 1993 and is scheduled as the venue for the Ryder Cup in 2014.

Hollinwell Close   A Nottinghamshire golf course designed by Willie Park junior, Hollinwell is 7,030 yards long. The club, which claims to be unique, was formed in 1887 by the Reverend A.H. Baynes with five enthusiasts playing golf on a recreation ground. They moved to Hollinwell at the beginning of the 20th century.

Hoylake Close   The Royal Liverpool golf course at Hoylake has become world famous since it was founded in 1869. It hosted the Open Championship ten times up until 1967, after which it was troubled by problems with space and transport. These have now been overcome. Hoylake also has an 18-hole municipal golf course which is 6,313 yards, par 70, and has about 300 members. It is described as a flat, windy, semi-links course with tricky fairways.

Hunstanton Way   An 18-hole par 72 links golf course, with views over the Wash in Norfolk, Hunstanton is 6,735 yards long and its club has about 675 members. Founded more than 100 years ago, it hosts many amateur championship events, including the English Ladies Championship.

Moor Park   Another famous golf club with an 'exclusive' reputation, this premier course is set within the 100-acre grounds of Moor Park mansion near Rickmansworth, Hertfordshire. The Grade I listed house, built between 1675-8 for the Duke of Monmouth, now contains the golf club with its 1,700 members. The High Course, par 72, and the West Course, par 69, are both 18 holes and designed by H.S. Colt.

Muirfield Drive   Having been home to the Honourable Company of Edinburgh Golfers since 1744, Muirfield Golf Club is recognised as the oldest in the world. An Open Championship course established in 1891, it is 6,673 yards long, par 70 and was designed by Harry Colt.

Penina Close   In Portugal, Penina Championship course is the Algarve's premier golf course. It was laid out on former rice fields by Sir Henry Cotton and involved the planting of 360,000 shrubs and trees, some of which are now 50 feet high. The result was regarded as a masterpiece. It was redesigned in 1994.

Portmarnock Close   In Ireland, Portmarnock Golf Club and course is on a small, windswept peninsula jutting into the Irish Sea, 20 minutes' drive from Dublin airport. With the sea on three sides and little in the way of natural windbreaks, the golfer needs warm clothes and an understanding of wind direction in order to survive. In its early days, there was no road to the club house, access being by boat or horse-and-cart at low tide. The course is laid out in serpentine fashion, with no two successive holes playing in the same direction.

Portrush Close   Royal Portrush Golf Club and course is in Northern Ireland. When the club was formed in 1888, it was known as the County Club, becoming the Royal County Club in 1892 when the Duke of York was its Patron. The name changed to Royal Portrush in 1895, when the Prince of Wales was Patron. The course was redesigned by H.S. Colt and opened in 1933 by the Lord Mayor of London. A new club house costing £1.5 million was opened in May 1999 by HRH Prince Andrew, Duke of York.

Prestwick Close   On the Ayrshire coast, which is home to many golf courses because of its suitable golfing terrain, Prestwick is half an hour's drive to the south-west of Glasgow, shares its boundary with Royal Troon course and is 20 minutes from Turnberry. It was founded in 1851 by the Earl of Eglinton who was its first captain. He put up the Eglinton Gold Medal prize which is still played for today. The course was designed by 'Old Tom Morris', who was keeper of the green, ball and club maker.

Pulborough Close   In West Sussex, Pulborough Golf Club has a membership of 850. The 18-hole course is par 68 and 6,221 yards long.

Richmond Close   Richmond Park golf course and golfing hotel, near Thetford in Norfolk, is set in 100 acres of parkland with the river Little Wissey running through it. There are also golf courses at Richmond in Surrey and Richmond, North Yorkshire.

Sunningdale Way   Just off the A30 at Sunningdale, Berkshire, there are two championship golf courses, both laid out on heathland. The Old par 70

Watling Street (A5) at Denbigh, looking north from Fenny Stratford.

course, designed by Willie Park, is the more famous and has 103 bunkers. The New par 71 course, designed by Harry Colt, was opened in 1923 with fewer trees and bunkers, but tighter fairways. The 1987 Walker Cup was played at Sunningdale, and in 1992 Nick Faldo won the European Open here.

Temple Close   Temple Golf Club at Maidenhead, Berkshire has 18 holes, is 6,207 yards, par 70, has about 480 members and was designed by Willie Park. In 2003 the club won the British Greenkeepers Award for the best environmentally managed course in the UK.

Turnberry Close   One of Scotland's leading golf complexes on the Ayrshire coast, Turnberry is a links course attached to a hotel. It began life 100 years ago on land owned by a railway company. During the Second World War it was used as an airfield, after which it was reconstructed by golf course architect, Mackenzie Ross. Running beside the sea, with sand dunes and craggy rocks, the course is 6,976 yards par 70. Turnberry hosted the British Open in 1977 and twice since.

Walton Heath   Walton Heath golf course and club near Reigate in Surrey was founded in 1903 by Sir Cosmo Bonsor and his son. It was designed by Herbert Fowler, a relative of the Bonsors. A new course was laid out by Fowler in 1907 and opened in 1913. James Braid was the club's first professional and remained there for 45 years.

Wentworth Way   Wentworth, Virginia Water in Surrey has three golf courses: the West, par 73, and the East, par 68, were laid out in 1924 and have hosted both professional and amateur events. The West course is now the permanent home of the World Matchplay Championship, held every

October and televised all over the world. The Edinburgh Course, 6,979 yards par 72, designed by John Jacobs with Gary Player and Bernard Gallacher, the resident pro,was opened in July 1990. A new nine-hole course has recently been added.

Windmill Hill Drive   At the highest point in Bletchley, where an ancient windmill once stood, Windmill Hill golf course was established in 1972 after Bletchley Urban District Council had acquired Windmill Hill Farm and Tattenhoe Farm and set aside 111 acres for the purpose. Former British Open champion, Henry Cotton, advised on the design of the 18-hole course, which was intended as an affordable one for Bletchley people. It is 6,720 yards long, par 73, has about 400 members and is considered a good course for beginners.

Witham Court   Of several golf courses in the Witham area of Essex, Benton Hall Golf Club has a challenging course beside the river Blackwater. Par 72, it has 18 holes over a yardage of 6,574. Braxted Park is a nine-hole, pay-and-play course in parkland surrounded by lakes.

RACECOURSE ESTATE

Aintree Close   Aintree is the Grand National course, near Liverpool. The first races held at Aintree in 1829 were over the flat, but ten years later, on 26 February 1839, the first Grand National was run over a stretch of ploughed field, with two hurdles and a stone wall to be jumped. Captain Martin Becher fell from his horse, Conrad, into the brook, which was thereafter named Becher's Brook. Owned by the Topham family between 1949 and 1973, Mrs Mirabel Topham built a new track in the early 1950s, as well as a motor-racing circuit on which Stirling Moss won his first Grand Prix in 1955.

Ascot Place   Ascot racecourse in Berkshire is famous for the Royal Ascot Race Meeting every June, which is a major event in the sporting calendar. The course was originally constructed at the order of Queen Anne in 1711 and, traditionally, the reigning monarch drives in an open carriage from Windsor castle to open Royal Ascot week.

Blaydon Close   Blaydon is a former racecourse on the outskirts of Gateshead. It was popular with the mining communities of Tyneside and is most famous for the song 'The Blaydon Races', written by Geordie Ridley and regarded as the National Anthem of Tyneside. The song's verses record some of the memorable occasions at the races. The last Blaydon races were held on 2 September 1916, but the meeting was abandoned when a riot broke out after a winning horse was disqualified. Today's Blaydon Races are athletics events.

Cartmel Close   Horse racing has taken place on Cartmel racecourse, Grange-over-Sands, Cumbria since 1845 and attracts a large attendance over its five days during the National Hunt season. Originally a flat racing course, by the early 20th century Cartmel had become a jumps-only venue. An amateur course until the 1960s, sponsorship, improved facilities and increased prize money now attracts the top quality horses and jockeys of today.

Cheltenham Gardens Cheltenham racecourse is the home of National Hunt racing and is possibly best known for the Cheltenham Gold Cup, first introduced in 1924. Only six horses have won the Gold Cup more than once. These famous names are Easter Hero (1928 and '29), Golden Miller (1932, '33, '34, '35 and '36), Cottage Rake (1948, '49 and '50), Arkle (1964, '65 and '66), L'Escargot (1970 and '71) and Best Mate (2002, '03 and '04). Sadly, Best Mate collapsed and died from a heart attack while racing at Exeter in October 2005. Cheltenham National Hunt Festival runs for three days in March.

Chepstow Drive In the Wye Valley, Chepstow racecourse is described as 'a unique and versatile leisure venue' near Bristol and Cardiff. As well as year-round horse racing, it hosts a wide range of public events, including a Sunday market, antiques fairs, a fun fair, an agricultural show, exhibitions and the Wye Dean car rally. It claims to have a friendly atmosphere and an impressive racing pedigree. Its racing calendar includes the Eurobet Welsh National, the Welsh Champion Hurdle and the Tote Silver Trophy.

Epsom Grove Epsom racecourse on the Epsom Downs in Surrey is the home of the Derby, run every June since 1780. A flat race introduced by the Earl of Derby, and the most prestigious of the English classics, it is a one-and-a-half mile race for three-year-olds. The Oaks, a flat race run over the same distance but for fillies only, takes place three days after the Derby. Another of the English Classics, the Oaks was first run in 1779 and was named after the 12th Earl of Derby's hunting lodge.

Fontwell Drive Fontwell Park racecourse on the edge of the Sussex Downs holds regular National Hunt meetings. It was laid out in 1924 in an unusual figure-of-eight circuit, with Fontwell House being purpose-built for race meetings. Many famous names have raced here, including Princess (now Queen) Elizabeth's Monarveen, who won here in 1949 and went on to finish fifth in that year's Grand National, which was won by Freebooter. In 2002 the Monarveen Handicap Chase was run at Fontwell. Fixtures have increased from four in 1924 to 18 in 2003 and, since 1991, Fontwell has been voted the best small racecourse in the south-east of England.

Hamilton Lane Hamilton Park racecourse near East Kilbride, Scotland has recently undergone a £2.5 million refurbishment. Racing has taken place at Hamilton since 1782 and on the present site since 1926. After suffering financial problems during the 1950s and '60s, it was saved in 1973 by a benefactor who formed a trust to secure the future of the course. Between April and September, Hamilton has 17 race fixtures a year, with the annual 'Saints and Sinners' race being a popular event.

Haydock Close   Haydock Park racecourse at Newton-le-Willows, Merseyside was created at the end of the 19th century. Prior to that, in the 1750s, the Newton Races had taken place on a course at Golborne Heath and, in memory of those days, the Old Newton Cup is still run over one-and-a-half miles in July. The main event of the season at Haydock is the Group 1 Stanley Leisure Sprint Cup.

Hexham Gardens   At Yarridge Heights above Hexham town, Hexham race-course has been home to National Hunt racing in Northumberland for more than a century. The site takes advantage of a natural amphitheatre of slop-ing grass which provides an excellent view of the course. In 1880, racing at Hexham was in decline so, encouraged by local enthusiasts, Charles William Chipchase Henderson restored the course at his own expense. Of the 18 fixtures held here, the main event is the Heart of All England Steeplechase Cup which was first presented in 1907 by 'the town and trade of Hexham'.

Huntingdon Crescent   The first meeting at Waterloo Meadows near Huntingdon was on Easter Monday 1886, when the first race was a three-mile steeplechase over what was little more than a point-to-point course. The number of meetings have gradually increased over the years to the 17 held today and the course is a venue for some of the best steeplechasers in the country. Among the famous names who have run here are Desert Orchid in 1991, and jockeys John Francome and Peter Scudamore. The main event in Huntingdon's racing calendar is the Peterborough Chase Day in the third week of November.

Kelso Close   In the Scottish Borders, Kelso offers high quality National Hunt racing. The first race meeting was held here in 1822 and lasted three days. The course has long received the patronage of the dukes of Roxburgh and the local farming community. The racecourse is in the Berrymoss area of Kelso.

Kempton Gardens   Kempton Park race meetings at Sunbury-on-Thames, Surrey were the first to be televised in the 1950s and 1960s. The history of the course begins in the 19th century, when businessman S.H. Hyde bought Kempton Manor and turned its parkland into a racecourse which opened in July 1878. The intention was to attract upper-class racegoers, particularly of the 'fair sex'. Between 1939 and 1946 it was used as a prisoner-of-war camp. Now Kempton Park is an all-year-round venue, with flat racing from March to September and National Hunt racing, opening with the Charisma Gold Cup, over the winter months. The highlight of the year is the Christmas meeting with the King George VI Chase on Boxing Day. Many famous horses are on Kempton's role of honour, including Desert Orchid who won the King George VI Chase four times. A memorial statue of Desert Orchid stands beside the paddock.

Newbury Court   Newbury racecourse in Berkshire hosts 28 days of top-class National Hunt and flat racing a year. Also, like most of today's racecourses, it derives an income from non-racing events such as exhibitions staged at its new conference and events centre. The Newbury course is set in 360 acres of Berkshire countryside and has a new state-of-the-art grandstand.

Sandown Court   Near Esher in Surrey, Sandown Park racecourse stands on the site of an Augustinian priory. In 1870, a lunatic asylum was proposed for the site, but Lt Col Owen Williams, a friend of the Prince of Wales, managed to secure it as a racecourse. The first races were held on 22 April 1875, the date still celebrated today as that of the Whitbread Gold Cup meeting, inaugurated by Col W.M. Whitbread in about 1957. With Kempton Park, racing from Sandown was first televised in 1947. A £3 million building programme was begun in 1972 and a year later the new grandstand was opened by the late Queen Elizabeth, the Queen Mother. A £23 million redevelopment was completed in 2002.

Thirsk Gardens   A North Yorkshire racecourse, Thirsk lies between the North Yorkshire Moors and the Dales. Horses have been raced here since 1740 and on the present course since 1855. The left-handed oval track over one-and-a-quarter miles has an undulating run-in of four furlongs on which sprint races are held. With 15 racing fixtures a year, Thirsk describes itself as 'country racing at its best' and is also a venue for conferences, craft fairs and exhibitions.

Wetherby Gardens   Wetherby racecourse in Yorkshire claims to have the finest jumping course in the north. A left-handed course with easy bends, Wetherby has a new £4 million Millennium Stand which was opened in February 2000, as well as refurbished hospitality facilities. Through the National Hunt season, there are 17 fixtures on the calendar.

Wincanton Hill   The first meeting at Wincanton racecourse in Somerset was held on Easter Monday 1927. Built on land attached to Kingwell Farm with financial backing from Lord Stalbridge, the course was requisitioned during the Second World War. Afterwards, it was bought and restored by ten local sportsmen and reopened in October 1945. Wincanton runs a programme of National Hunt racing from October to May. The Lord Stalbridge Memorial Cup is run on Boxing Day.

THE RIVERS ESTATE

Avon Grove   Of several river Avons in the United Kingdom, one rises near Naseby, Northamptonshire and flows 96 miles south-west to the Severn at Tewkesbury. Another, in south-west England, flows 75 miles from Gloucestershire to the Severn estuary at Avonmouth. A third river Avon, in southern England, flows 60 miles from the Wiltshire/Berkshire border, through Salisbury to the English Channel.

Calder Vale   There are three Calder rivers. One has its source on Calder (or Cold) Fell in the Cumbrian hills, from where it flows south-westwards down through the village of Calder Vale on its way to the sea at Seascale. Another, rising in the Pennine hills, flows eastwards through Hebden Bridge, Dewsbury and Wakefield, where old mills and workers' cottages are monuments to the river's importance in the development of Yorkshire's woollen industry. The third, in Scotland, rises as the Calder Water in north Ayrshire, flows east into Renfrewshire and widens to become the River Calder, then continues south-east to flow into Castle Semple Loch.

Cam Court   The river Cam is an East Anglian river, flowing for about 40 miles from the borders of Hertfordshire and Cambridgeshire north of Royston, through Cambridge and across the fens to just south of Ely, where it joins the river Great Ouse.

Clyde Place   The river Clyde, famed for its Clydebank shipyards, rises within a mile of the River Tweed in the southern uplands of Scotland. It flows over the hills to the west and travels 106 miles to the sea at Glasgow. Clydesdale, through which it flows, is a rich valley noted for fruit growing and the Clydesdale draught horse.

Derwent Drive   The Derwent is the largest river of the Peak District and a major tributary of the Trent, which it joins just south of Derby. It rises on the eastern flank of Bleaklow and is 50 miles long. The upper reaches flow through steep-sided moorland and feed three Derwent reservoirs on the way to the beautiful Hope Valley, then through the grounds of Chatsworth and on to Matlock and Cromford, where the water powered Arkwright's cotton mills. Then it turns away to Derby.

Eden Walk   High in the Pennines of eastern Cumbria, three springs converge to form the source of the river Eden, which flows north-west through the fertile Vale of Eden to Appleby, on its 90-mile journey to its estuary in the Solway Firth. The river Eden is a designated Site of Special Scientific Interest because of the abundance of wild flora, fauna and natural habitats, both within the river and along its course, which are worthy of conservation.

Esk Way   There are two river Esks. One begins life at Westerdale in the North Yorkshire Moors, where a series of becks known as Esklets merge to form the Esk river. From here it falls and splashes eastwards, across open moorland and through Eskdale to the sea at Whitby. The other river Esk has its source on Scafell Pike in the Cumbrian mountains and flows westwards through another Eskdale to the sea at Ravenglass.

Humber Way   The Humber river is formed from the confluence of the rivers Ouse and Trent on the border between Lincolnshire and South Yorkshire. A wide river, it forms the Humber estuary and flows for 40 miles into the North Sea at Spurn Head. Immingham docks, the fishing port of Grimsby and the Europort at Hull, with its ferry service between Rotterdam and Zeebrugge, mean that the Humber is busy with shipping. The Humber Bridge, opened in 1981 and linking north and south Humberside, is the longest single-span suspension bridge in the world.

Isis Walk   The Isis is the name given to the section of the Thames which lies within the city of Oxford. Isis was an Egyptian goddess believed to have healing powers and represented the perfect mother. Rowing and pleasure boating take place on the Isis.

Kennet Drive and Kennet Place   The Kennet rises from various springs in the chalk rocks of Wiltshire's Marlborough Downs, from where it flows through Hungerford and Newbury in Berkshire before joining the Thames at Reading. As one of the best chalk rivers in Britain, with many rare plants and animals along much of its course, the Kennet is a Site of Special Scientific Interest.

Lovatt Drive   The Lovatt is the name given to that section of the river Ouzel which flows within the parish boundary of Newport Pagnell and a few miles south of the town.

Mersey Way and Mersey Close   The Mersey rises in the Pennines and flows 70 miles to the Irish Sea at Liverpool. Several docks were built at Liverpool by Thomas Stears in 1717 and by the 19th century pollution from Lancashire's textile industry and the dyeing and bleaching processes had destroyed the water quality and with it the fishing industry. In the 1980s, the Mersey Basin Campaign achieved a clean-up and fish are returning to the river.

Nene Drive   The Nene rises from sources near Naseby, Badby and Yelvertoft in Northamptonshire, and from Northampton flows in a north-easterly direction, 91 miles to the Wash. Navigable, it passes through stone-built villages and Cambridgeshire farmland before crossing the wide expanse of the Cambridgeshire Fens.

Otter Close   The river Otter flows from its source in the Culm Valley through east Devon, giving its name to Otterton, Up Ottery and Ottery St Mary, where the poet Samuel Taylor Coleridge was born at the vicarage. Numerous trout inhabit the river and the Otter estuary at Budleigh Salterton is a haven for thousands of birds. It is a nature reserve and a Site of Special Scientific Interest.

Ouzel Close   The river Ouzel, also known as the Lovatt, rises south-east of Leighton Buzzard and flows south of Bletchley to Walton, then up the eastern side of Milton Keynes to Newport Pagnell. The Ouzel is mentioned in Domesday Book as having several valuable mills along its course, including Caldecotte Mill, Water Eaton, Simpson, Fox Milne, the Woolstones and Willen.

Ribble Crescent   The source of the Ribble is high in the Pennines above Kirkby Lonsdale. It flows through Ribchester and Preston before reaching the sea at Lytham, Lancashire.

Severn Way   The Severn is Britain's longest river at 220 miles. The source is a boggy pool oozing out of the ground in the Cambrian mountains, 2,000 feet above sea level. It is crossed by 100 bridges on the journey to its mouth in the Bristol Channel which has the second highest tidal range in the world. In the 18th century, vessels were able to sail up the Severn as far as Welshpool.

Stour Close   Of four river Stours, that in Suffolk, flowing through 'Constable Country', is possibly the first to come to mind. Featured in many of Constable's paintings, it flows through the reed beds of the fens to Dedham Lock and Flatford Mill on its way to the North Sea at Harwich. The river Stour in the West Midlands flows through Stourbridge, Kidderminster and Stourport, where it joins the Severn. The Great Stour, Little Stour and East Stour are all Kentish rivers flowing from the North Downs to the English Channel at Pegwell Bay. The fourth river Stour flows from Sturminster in north Dorset, past Blandford and Bournemouth to the English Channel at Christchurch.

Tattenhoe Lane   This is a section of the old lane which led from Buckingham Road, Bletchley to the village of Tattenhoe.

Tay Road   The Tay is the longest river in Scotland and offers superb salmon fishing. It rises in the Grampians and flows through wooded valleys to Dunkeld, and through Perth before entering the Firth of Tay and the North Sea at Dundee after a 120-mile journey.

Tees Way   The source of the Tees is in the northern Pennines at Tees Head, where a stone with the inscription 'B/T' marks the 'birth of the Tees'. From here it flows down through Teesdale, Barnard Castle and on to the sea at Tees Bay beyond Stockton-on-Tees. The river provides coarse fishing and the area of Teesside became heavily industrialised with iron and steel works during the Industrial Revolution.

Thames Close   'Old Father Thames', Southern England's principal river, rises in the Cotswolds near Cirencester and flows mainly east-south-east through Oxford, Reading and London to the North Sea at the Nore, a sandbank near Sheerness. Its upper, non-tidal reaches are tranquil and beautiful while, throughout history, the Thames estuary and the Port of London have been busy with shipping and huge amounts of cargo, making the river the most economically important in the United Kingdom.

The Don   There are two river Dons, one in Yorkshire, flowing from Bramwell aqueduct near Sheffield and through Doncaster to Goole, where it joins the Ouse. The other is in Scotland and begins in the Grampians to wind its way down to the sea at Aberdeen. This is another salmon and trout river with sections of fast-flowing stream and rocky pools alternating with stretches of slow, deep and tranquil waters. There is a hatchery at the Mill of Newe, which was once a meal mill.

Trent Road   A river of central England, the Trent flows south-east from Staffordshire and north-east through Nottingham before joining the Ouse to form the Humber estuary. It is the main river of the Midlands and was heavily commercialised during the Industrial Revolution. It is linked to the Mersey by a canal and its overall distance is 170 miles.

Tweed Drive   The river Tweed in Scotland is renowned for its salmon fishing. Over a course of about 90 miles, around 10,000 fish are produced per year. The river's source is in the Southern Uplands in the west of Scotland, from where it flows easterly and is approximately 100 miles from beginning to end. The lower part of the river is the border between Scotland and England. The Tweed is also famed for its swans, which are permanent residents of Berwick-on-Tweed.

Tyne Square   The river Tyne, in north-east England, begins west of Hexham, where the North Tyne, flowing from Kielder, and the South Tyne, flowing from Alston Moor, join to form the Tyne, which flows into the sea at Tynemouth. Tyneside was Britain's first industrialised region, having been developed some time before the Industrial Revolution. Its shipbuilding industry has declined in recent years. Many bridges cross the river, including the Gateshead Millennium bridge and the Tyne bridge, opened in October 1928, between Newcastle and Gateshead.

Wye Close   From its source in the Plynlimon Hills, the Wye flows 130 miles through mid-Wales and the Marches to join the Severn at Beachley in the Forest of Dean near Chepstow. Noted for its tranquil waters and beautiful scenery, the Wye also has salmon fisheries.

THE SAINTS ESTATE

St Aidans Close   Aidan was an Irish saint who died in AD 626. Noted for his love of animals and dislike of hunting, he is said to have miraculously made a stag invisible to save it from the pursuing hounds and his symbol in Christian art is a stag. Born in Connaught, he came to Wales for a time before returning to Ireland where he built a monastery. His feast day is 31 January.

St Andrews Road   St Andrew is the patron saint of Scotland and of Russia, with a feast day on 30 November. He was a fisherman working with his brother, Simon Peter, and a disciple of John the Baptist before becoming the first of the 12 apostles of Jesus. Andrew was also the first Christian missionary. He preached in Scythia, Greece and Byzantium before meeting his death by crucifixion on an X-shaped cross at Patra in AD 60.

St Catherines Avenue   Of several St Catherines, Catherine of Alexandria was a fourth-century Christian. She challenged the emperor over the persecution of Christians and was sentenced to be 'broken' on the wheel. The wheel is said to have been shattered by an angel and she was beheaded instead. This legend gave rise to the 'catherine wheel' firework. St Catherine of Sienna (1347-80) was an Italian mystic and nun who devoted her life to caring for the sick and the poor and to contemplation. She is said to have received the stigmata on her body in 1375. Her feast day is 30 April. St Catherine of Genoa (1447-1510) was an Italian mystic from a noble family. She had a religious conversion when she was 26 and devoted her life to caring for the sick. Her feast day is 15 September.

St Clements Drive   In the late first century AD, Clement I was the fourth Bishop of Rome. He was known for his writings condemning the evils of jealousy and propounding the need for tolerance, compassion and duty of care between the different levels of human society. He is believed to have been greatly respected by the Church as a wise arbitrator and legislator.

St Davids Road   The patron saint of Wales with a feast day on 1 March, David was born in Cardigan in the late fifth century. He founded 12 monasteries, setting up communities of severe deprivation in which speech was not allowed unless absolutely necessary. The monks tilled the land and lived on a diet of bread, vegetables and salt. His emblem is a dove.

St Georges Road   The guardian saint of England, Portugal and soldiers, St George's cult was brought to England by crusaders returning from Palestine where, it is believed, he was martyred during the Emperor Diocletian's rule. St George was a crusading knight in Libya, where the people were being terrorised by a man-eating beast. George said he would slay the dragon if the people would believe in Jesus as their Saviour and agree to be baptised. So many legends surround St George that some sceptics argue he never existed, although it is generally believed that a knight called George did suffer Christian martyrdom in Palestine in about AD 303.

St Johns Road   One of the 12 apostles of Jesus and a Gospel writer, John was the son of Zebedee and brother of James. He was present at a number of events in the life of Jesus and is thought to be the disciple 'whom Jesus loved', attending the crucifixion. It is believed that St John escaped martyrdom and died at Ephesus. His feast day is 27 December.

St Marys Avenue   Of several saints called Mary, the choice when naming this street was probably St Mary the Blessed Virgin Mother of Jesus. Central to the Christian faith, nothing is known about her life other than what is written in the four Gospels of the Bible. According to Christian tradition, she was the daughter of Joachim and Ann, spent much of her childhood in the temple and devoted her life to the service of God. The given date of her death is AD 63.

St Matthews Court   Matthew was working for the Romans as a tax collector before he became an apostle of Jesus. He wrote the first of the four New Testament Gospels, originally intending it for his fellow Jews. He preached in Judaea, Ethiopia and Persia and suffered martyrdom. St Matthew's feast day is 21 September and his emblem is a man with wings.

St Patricks Way   St Patrick, patron saint of Ireland, lived around AD 385-

461 and is believed to have been born in Wales. According to legend, when he was 16 he was abducted by Irish pirates, taken to Ireland and sold to an Antrim chief. Six years later he escaped, went to France and became a monk. At the age of 45, he was ordained a bishop and returned to Ireland as a missionary, intent upon converting his old master and other Irish chiefs to Christianity. In about AD 454, St Patrick established his see at Armagh, where he is believed to have been buried following his death at Saul (now Saulpatrick). His feast day is 17 March and his emblems are the shamrock and snakes.

St Pauls Road   Born Saul of Tarsus of Jewish parents, the young St Paul trained as a rabbi and a tent-maker in Jerusalem. An ardent Pharisee who persecuted Christians, he was on the road to Damascus when he had a vision of the crucified Jesus and was converted to Christianity. He made many mission journeys across Asia Minor and as far as Corinth, before finally reaching Rome in AD 62, only to be imprisoned for two years before being executed under Nero. Many of the Bible's New Testament Epistles are attributed to St Paul.

Saint Thomas Aquinas RC Combined School   His family was so opposed to Thomas becoming a Dominican monk that they held him captive for 15 months to dissuade him. After studying in Paris and Cologne he became a lecturer, and in 1272 he founded a school in Naples. His teachings have become influential, his mission being to prove the existence of God to non-believers. His writings are recognised as intellectual masterpieces, even by those who disagree with them. He wrote: 'I cannot understand how a person can even smile if he is in a state of mortal sin.' He died in 1274.

GRANBY

In the mid-18th century, the notorious Denbigh Hall *public house became known as the* Marquis of Granby, *a popular name for inns after John Manners, Marquis of Granby (1721-70) became a national hero. A commissioned officer during the Jacobite Rebellion of '45, he reached the rank of major-general in the Duke of Cumberland's staff and in 1760 redeemed the cavalry's reputation with a resounding victory at Warburg. Walpole called Granby 'the mob's hero' and he was appointed Master General of the Ordnance. Most of Granby is a business park.*

Granby Court   This corner of the business park has residential accommodation.

Drew Court   This possibly refers to Jane Drew of architects Maxwell Fry, who designed the alterations to Walton Hall and new buildings for the Open University. With Fry, she had a reputation for pioneering the Bauhaus style in England in the 1930s and later collaborated with Le Corbusier on Chandigarh, the 'city of silver' and capital of the Punjab. Milton Keynes mosque is in this corner of Granby.

Peverel Drive   *Peverel of the Peake* was the name of a stagecoach regularly seen on Watling Street and it no doubt called at the coaching inns at Little Brickhill, Fenny and Stony Stratford en route.

MOUNT FARM

Developed in the late 1960s and early 1970s on land containing old gravel pits, this area presumably had at some time a Mount Farm. The gravel pits are now an attractive lake, teeming with wildfowl and surrounded by grassland. A variety of companies operate from the sprawl of light industrial units.

Auckland Park   The founder and chairman of Terrapin Ltd was Harry Bolt, a New Zealander. In 1989 he cut the first soil of this business park which was then named after Auckland, New Zealand. Fittingly, the names 'New Zealand' and 'Van Diemen's Land' (Tasmania) appear on a post-1778 map and list of field names in the Bletchley area.

Bond Avenue   Takes its name from Bond Estates Ltd, a subsidiary of Terrapin group of companies which operate from here.

Bramley Road   Albert Bramley was a coal and lime merchant at Simpson and a first member of Fenny Stratford Urban District Council when it was formed in 1895. Bramley became Council Chairman in 1900 and served on the UDC for over 20 years.

Clarke Road   Named after Gregory Odell Clarke, who had his own wharf by the canal at Fenny Stratford, a limekiln on three acres of land off Aylesbury Street, and a brickworks. Between 1820 and 1870, he was one of Fenny Stratford's busiest citizens, being a coal, timber, slate and iron merchant as well as brick and tile maker. After his death his son, Edward Clarke, expanded the company, opening brick yards in Simpson, Water Eaton, Woburn Sands and Ridgmont.

Dawson Road   Believed to have taken its name from the Dawson Freight company which operated from here before moving to new premises in Tongwell.

Grove Ash   Possibly there was a grove of ash trees here.

Mount Avenue   There is a slight hill, or mount here, which would have prompted the original name of this area.

Ward Road   There are two very valid candidates for this name. Most probable is Mr C.A. Ward, who was chief surveyor of Percy Bilton Ltd, a construction company operating in Bletchley for several years. The other Mr Ward was foreman for Beacon Brushes Ltd, which also occupied large premises here for many years.

OLD BLETCHLEY

Beechcroft Road   This is probably the name of a field, or an area where beech trees grew.

Bletchley Park   The home of the Leon family, the Bletchley Park estate once covered a square mile from Watling Street to Shenley Road and from Buckingham Road to the old Rickley Lane. When Lady Leon died in 1936, the estate was auctioned off. The house and immediate grounds were bought by a local developer, Hubert Faulkner, who built Wilton Avenue. The Ministry of Works bought the house and grounds in 1939 for the Foreign Office and, as we now know, it became 'Station X', the secret location for the decoding of German military cyphers during the Second World War.

Buckingham Road   This is the old road which led from Watling Street, through Bletchley to Buckingham, the historic county town superseded by Aylesbury.

Cathay Close   This name seems to be fancifully paired with Gilbert Close. Cathay was the name used by Marco Polo for the area around northern China which 16th-century navigators attempted to discover by means of a north-west or north-east passage. The name derives from a 10th-century Manchurian Tartar kingdom called Khitai.

Bletchley Park, once home of Sir Herbert Leon, today Bletchley Park Museum.

Church Green Road   Leading to the parish church of St Mary, originally built in the 12th century with several additions taking place between the 13th and 15th centuries. It was last restored in the 19th century.

Church Walk   A footpath, still running to join Church Green Road, once ran from here all the way to St Mary's church.

Corrigan Close   Not found.

Cottingham Grove   This is named after an ancient track which led to Cottenham brook, which was used as the town's main outlet for sewage.

Rectory Cottages, Church Green Road. The oldest house in Milton Keynes, listed in 1447, moved to its present site in 1618. Its barn has a 15th-century hammerbeam roof of exceptional interest.

Craigmore Avenue   No true explanation has been found, but one local resident believes it was named after Craig, the son of a Bletchley councillor called Moore, while another suggests that Craig is the grandson of Horace Tranfield, developer of the road.

Elmers Park   Named after William Elmer of Beachampton, near Stony Stratford, whose endowment provided for the building of a school there in 1648. It catered for the free education of about sixty boys, and a few girls who had to pay. Between 1692 and 1695, it was attended by Browne Willis, who went on from there to Westminster School. It has since become a private house.

The Elmers, Bletchley.

Gilbert Close   Adjacent to Cathay Close, this seems to be a fanciful choice of name and is believed to refer to Sir Humphrey Gilbert (1537-83), an English navigator who, in 1576, wrote a *Discourse to prove a passage by the Northwest to Cataya* (Cathay). In 1583 he discovered Newfoundland and on the voyage home was drowned with all aboard when his ship, *The Squirrel*, sank.

Grange Road   The Grange is marked on the original *Plan for*

Milton Keynes, published by Milton Keynes Development Corporation in the late 1960s, on the corner of Buckingham Road and Newton Road. It was the home of Major John Whiteley (see Whiteley Crescent) and formed a small estate until the house was demolished and the land used for development. Only the lodge remains at the corner of the Poets Estate.

Mellish Court This is a tower block built in 1966 and named after Robert Mellish, Minister for Housing and Local Government, who opened the building in December that year.

Newton Road The road from Bletchley to Newton Longville.

Orchard Close There was once an orchard here, shown on a 1771 map of field enclosures.

Park Gardens Built in the gardens of Bletchley Park.

Rickley Lane Rickley Lane was the name of a very old track which ran from Watling Street to the great house at Salden near Mursley, home of Sir John Fortescue. Skirting Rickley Wood, it was a major road in its day, but by 1766 was suffering from neglect as none of the parishes would accept responsibility for its repair, and it disappeared. On a map of 1813, Rickley Lane is shown as a track running for about 110 yards due south from Watling Street and in 1950 it was still just visible as a cart track across the fields.

Roche Gardens Off Whalley Drive, this refers to Roche Abbey, which lies in the deep valley of Maltby Beck, North Yorkshire. Founded in 1147 by a colony of Cistercian monks from Newminster Abbey, Northumberland, it was 25 years before they began building the impressive stone abbey of which today's ruins were a part. It was completed by the end of the 12th century, with further buildings added on the other side of the beck during the 13th century. By the time of the dissolution of the monasteries, 400 years later, there were only 14 monks and four novices left to witness its terrible destruction.

Selbourne Avenue No explanation can be found.

Shenley Road This is the old road from Bletchley to the villages of Shenley Church End and Shenley Brook End.

Sherwood Drive Named after R.L. Sherwood who was appointed Clerk to the Bletchley Urban District Council in July 1932. He served the town for 30 years.

South Lawne The archaic meaning of a lawn was an open space between woodlands. An enclosure called South Lawne is shown on a 1718 map as part of Bletchley Park Manor estate.

The Elms Frank Markham in his *History of Milton Keynes and District* refers to the 'many beautiful trees' in Bletchley Park, and there were probably elm trees on this spot.

The Grove   As this was part of Bletchley Park estate, no doubt a grove, or small plantation of trees, grew here.

Travis Grove   Commander Edward 'Jumbo' Travis was head of the Naval Section of the Government Code and Cypher School at Bletchley Park and deputy to the Chief Commander, Alastair Denniston. As such he was the main adviser to the government on what type of codes and cyphers to use. He was knighted in 1942 and succeeded Denniston as head of Bletchley Park.

Wellington Place   Site of the Territorial Army centre. The Duke of Wellington was the victor of the Battle of Waterloo (18 June 1815) which ended the Napoleonic wars. It was on Wellington's recommendation that George IV elevated the Marquess of Buckingham to Duke of Buckingham and Chandos and Marquess of Chandos in February 1822.

Whaddon Way   This is the old road, once on the outskirts of Bletchley, running from Watling Street to Whaddon.

Whalley Drive   A long drive from the rear of Bletchley Park and skirting the Abbeys Estate, this road takes its name from Whalley Abbey in Lancashire. A Cistercian monastery originally founded in 1178 in Stanlow, Cheshire, it was re-established at Whalley in 1296 after a fire destroyed the abbey at Stanlow. Whalley was also the name of one of the most famous charities which existed in this area during the 17th century, an apprenticing charity, which introduced young men to various trades in different places, including London and Kent.

Whiteley Crescent   Major John Whiteley was a popular Bletchley man who lived at The Grange. He became Conservative MP for Buckingham in 1937, but his political career was interrupted by the Second World War and, as Lt Col Commanding the Royal Bucks Yeomanry RA, he volunteered for war service and was actively engaged until killed in action on 4 July 1943 in an air crash over Gibraltar. The Polish Prime Minister, General Sikorski, and Col Victor Cazalet MP in the same aircraft, were also killed.

Wilton Avenue   Providing access to Bletchley Park and Wilton Hall, which was built by Hubert Faulkner in 1939, both hall and

St Mary's parish church, Bletchley dates from the 14th century.

Effigy of Baron Grey in St Mary's church, Bletchley.

avenue take their name from the Barons Grey de Wilton, lords of the manors of Bletchley and Water Eaton from the Middle Ages to the 17th century. Reginald de Grey married Maud, heiress of Hugh de Longchamp of Wilton Castle in Herefordshire, and was created the first Baron de Wilton in about 1250.

THE POETS ESTATE

Brooke Close   Rupert Brooke (1887-1915), remembered as one of 'the war poets' who wrote moving poems about their experiences in the First World War, died a commissioned officer on Skyros on his way to the Dardanelles and was buried there. His best-known poem is probably *Grantchester*, describing where he lived in Cambridgeshire.

Browning Crescent   Robert Browning (1812-89) was the son of a clerk in the Bank of England. His mother was German-Scottish. His best-known work is *The Pied Piper of Hamelin*, and he married Elizabeth Barrett (1806-61), also a poet.

Burns Road   Robert Burns (1759-96), Scotland's greatest poet, was born in Ayrshire, son of a cotter who moved from one unprofitable farm to another but, determined that his sons would be educated, sent them to the local school at Alloway Mill. He adapted his verse to every aspect of Scottish life which came his way and wrote both in his native dialect and in 18th-century English. On his birthday, 25 January, Burns Night is celebrated by Scottish people all over the world.

Byron Close   George Gordon, 6th Baron Byron of Rochdale (1788-1824) was born in London, son of a squanderer, Captain John Byron, known as 'Mad Jack', and Catherine Gordon of Gight, a Scottish heiress who was equally reckless. Little wonder that Byron himself became famously known as 'mad, bad and dangerous to know'. Nevertheless, he was a leading light of the Romantic movement in poetry. As well as many shorter poems, which include *She Walks in Beauty* and *So, We'll Go No More a Roving,* Byron wrote several epics such as *The Siege of Corinth, Childe Harold's Pilgrimage* and *Don Juan.*

Chaucer Road   Geoffrey Chaucer (*c.*1343-1400) was the son of a London vintner and innkeeper. In 1357, he was a page in the service of the Duke of Clarence, and later on was among the king's household and known as 'our beloved yeoman'. In 1386 he was made a knight of the shire of Kent. Best known for his *Canterbury Tales,* Chaucer also wrote *The Parliament of Fowls, The House of Fame* and *Troilus and Cressida.*

Coleridge Close   Samuel Taylor Coleridge (1772-1834), poet, critic and philosopher of Romanticism, was the youngest son of the vicar of Ottery St Mary, Devon, and had been expected to follow his father into the Church. However, his somewhat ethereal and temperamental nature led him into the company of poets and he formed a close friendship with William and Dorothy Wordsworth. Best known among his works are *The Rime of the Ancient Mariner, Frost at Midnight, Christabel* and *Kubla Khan,* the last said to have been written under the influence of opium, to which he became addicted.

Keats Way   John Keats (1795-1821) was the son of the manager of a livery stables in Moorfields, who died when John was eight. His mother remarried, but died of tuberculosis when he was fourteen. Keats started writing poetry in 1814 while he was an apothecary's apprentice. He studied at Guy's Hospital but gave up thoughts of a medical career in favour of poetry. He is well-known for his odes – *On a Grecian Urn, To a Nightingale, To Psyche,* and others. His poems include *The Eve of St Agnes, The Eve of St Mark* and longer works such as *Endymion* and *Hyperion.* Keats died in Rome in February 1821 of tuberculosis, aged only 26.

Kipling Road   Rudyard Kipling (1865-1936) was born in Bombay, the son of an author and illustrator. He was sent to school in England in 1871, but returned to India, where he worked as a journalist. In 1907, he was the first English writer to be awarded the Nobel Prize for Literature. He is best known for his tales for children – *The Jungle Book, Just So Stories* and *Puck of Pook's Hill* – and also for his adult masterpiece, *Kim,* his novel of India.

Masefield Grove   John Edward Masefield (1878-1967) had an idyllic childhood in Herefordshire, which later influenced much of his work. His mother died in 1884 and the relatives who cared for him sent him to train in the Merchant Navy when he was 13 years old. He suffered badly from sea-sickness, had a breakdown and deserted when he was 17. For a time he was a vagrant in America and started writing poetry. His works are prolific and by 1930 he was Poet Laureate. In 1935 he was awarded the Order of Merit.

Milton Grove   John Milton (1608-74) was born in Bread Street, Cheapside. His father was a scrivener and composer of music. Milton's unique style is powerful and resonant, with use of strong imagery and Latin syntax. Apart from his famous *Paradise Lost*, there is the elegy *Lycidas*, the masque *Comus* and a sonnet on his blindness. A learned man, steeped in the Classics and religion, he moved to Horton, Buckinghamshire in 1635, and in 1665, during the plague years, was living in Chalfont St Giles.

Shelley Drive   Percy Bysshe Shelley (1792-1822) was another of the great Romantic poets. The eldest son of the MP for Horsham, he was born at Field Place, Sussex. He was educated at Eton, where he was bullied and taunted as 'Mad Shelley'. After the breakup of his first marriage to 16-year-old Harriet Westbrook, he eloped with Mary Godwin (better known as Mary Shelley, author of *Frankenstein*) whom he married after Harriet had drowned herself in the Serpentine. Among Shelley's many works are *Prometheus Unbound, Ode to the West Wind* and *Adonais*, which he wrote on the death of his great friend, John Keats. Shelley's own death occurred a year later in August 1822 when, returning after a visit to Byron in Livorno, Italy, his small boat capsized and he was drowned.

Tennyson Grove   Alfred, Lord Tennyson (1st Baron Tennyson) (1809-92) was born in Somersby Rectory, Lincolnshire, fourth son of the rector. His childhood at the rectory was miserable. His father was an unhappy man who drank and became violent, causing his mother to leave, and Alfred later suffered from melancholia, which is reflected in his early poems. From about 1850, when he made a happy marriage, his life and his finances improved and so did his output of poetry. He succeeded Wordsworth as Poet Laureate in 1850. Although he wrote many lengthy works such as *The Lady of Shalott*, Tennyson is probably best known for *The Charge of the Light Brigade, Blow, Bugle Blow* and *Maud*.

Wordsworth Drive   William Wordsworth (1770-1850) was born at Cockermouth, Cumbria, son of an attorney. Of the Romantic school of poetry, much of his verse reflects his life in and love of the Lake District. Apart from the well-known *Daffodils,* his works include *The Lucy Poems, The Excursion* and his beautiful epic, *The Prelude*.

WEST BLETCHLEY

Archers Wells   'Great Archers Wells' and 'Upper, Middle and Lower Archers Wells' were the names of four fields shown on a survey of arable and pasture lands in 1718.

Banburies Close   Banburies were used to set Enigma messages in depth with each other. The 1944 *Bletchley Park Cryptographic Dictionary* is believed to have been edited by James Wyllie, who worked in the research section at Bletchley Park. In it, a Banbury is defined as 'a sheet or strip of paper having vertical alphabets printed across its width at equal intervals on which a cipher message can be reproduced by punching out the consecutive letters of the text in consecutive columns, designed to facilitate the placing of messages in depth'.

Beaverbrook Court   William Maxwell Aitken, 1st Baron Beaverbrook (1879-1964) was a Canadian-born British politician and newspaper tycoon. He became Private Secretary to Bonar Law and was knighted in 1911. Under Lloyd George he was Minister of Information, and in 1919 he launched into journalism, taking over the *Daily Express*, founding the *Sunday Express* in 1921 and buying the *Evening Standard* in 1929. During the Second World War, Beaverbrook was made Minister of Supply, Lord Privy Seal and Lend-Lease administrator in the USA.

Bushy Close   This probably denotes an area of bushy shrubland, or an area of wild, uncultivated land, on which this close was built.

Calluna Drive   *Calluna vulgaris* is the Latin name for the common heather which grows on heaths and moorlands, often covering vast areas of land with its pale purple flowers. It probably was abundant here before the site was developed.

Cheynes Walk   This may have been named in connection with William Sparke, who in 1616 was rector of St Mary's church, Bletchley and chaplain to the Duke of Buckingham. He was forced to resign his post after he got into debt, but became rector of Chenies (named after the Cheyne family) near Amersham, Bucks, where he died in 1641 and is buried. In the 16th century, the Cheynes conveyed their manor to the Russells, earls and dukes of Bedford.

Greenlaw Place   Greenlaw is a small town on the river Blackadder in the Scottish Border county of Berwickshire, not far from Melrose Abbey. In Scotland, a law is a rounded or conical hill.

Highfield Close   Probably named after one of the fields belonging to Home Farm.

Home Close   Past the junction of Sherwood Drive and Whalley Drive, Home Close is the old name of a field shown near Home Farm on Milton Keynes Development Corporation's original Plan.

Kerria Place   Kerria is a genus of deciduous shrub grown for its showy yellow flowers.

Lintlaw Place   Lintlaw is a small Scottish Border town to the north-west of Berwick-on-Tweed.

Spenlows Road   'Spenlows Meadow' was the name of a field shown on a survey of arable and pasture land in 1718.

The Linx   'Lower Linx', 'Middle Linx' and 'Upper Linx' were fields named on a survey of arable and pasture lands in 1718.

Whaddon Way   This was the old road leading to Whaddon from Watling Street.

THE ABBEYS ESTATE

Bolton Close   The romantic setting of the ruins of Bolton Abbey near Skipton, North Yorkshire has inspired Wordsworth, the poet, and Turner and Landseer, the artists. The estate now centred round Bolton Priory, founded in 1154, is owned by the Chatsworth Settlement and includes the Yorkshire home of the Duke and Duchess of Devonshire.

Buckfast Avenue   Buckfast Abbey in Devon is two miles from Ashburton. A Benedictine monastery founded in 1018 by King Cnut, it was suppressed by Henry VIII's dissolution of the monasteries in 1539, but was the only medieval monastery to be restored to its former use after the Reformation. It was refounded in 1882 and the abbey church rebuilt by the monks themselves. Buckfast has a long and fascinating history which is revealed to visitors shown round the Abbey by today's community of monks.

Cleeve Crescent   Cleeve Abbey at Washford, Somerset is a monastic site where a unique set of cloister buildings has been preserved, including the refectory with a timber roof. Built in the 13th century, this Cistercian abbey was saved from complete destruction at the dissolution by being turned into a house and then a farm.

Dorchester Avenue   On the river Thame, Oxfordshire, Dorchester Abbey was originally built in the late 12th century for Augustinian canons. The original lead font and 13th-century stained-glass windows still survive, as does much of the building, which escaped the worst of Henry VIII's destructive forces during the dissolution.

Furness Crescent   The beautiful red sandstone ruins of Furness Abbey near Barrow-in-Furness, Cumbria are now owned by English Heritage. Founded in 1123 by Stephen, later King of England, Furness was once a wealthy abbey, originally belonging to the order of Savigny and then to the Cistercians.

Glastonbury Close   Glastonbury Abbey in Somerset is traditionally believed to have been the first Christian sanctuary in Britain and is the legendary burial place of King Arthur, although this has been disputed. Evidence suggests that there may have been a monastery here in AD 600. A Norman abbey was destroyed by fire in 1184 and the extensive buildings of a new one, begun at the end of the 12th century, had only just been completed by 1539 when they were ransacked by Henry VIII's dissolution of the monasteries. The Abbot Whiting was hanged on Glastonbury Tor. In 1560 the abbey became home to a colony of weavers. Today the ruins are preserved in a 36-acre site in the centre of Glastonbury.

Hinton Court   Hinton Charterhouse, a 13th-century Carthusian priory, lies in ruins a few miles south of Bath in Somerset. It is the second oldest Carthusian house in England and part of the priory, lodge and gatehouse are now part of Hinton House, an 18th-century mansion. The village of Hinton Charterhouse stands in the wooded countryside a mile away.

Melrose Avenue   The substantial ruin of the Cistercian abbey of Melrose is one of the four Scottish Border abbeys built during the 12th century by David I. During the Border wars it suffered repeated destructive attacks and was rebuilt in the 15th century, only to be destroyed again in 1543 by English raids. It is believed to be the burial place of the heart of Robert the Bruce.

Neath Crescent   Neath Abbey, near Swansea, South Wales, was founded by Richard de Granville in 1130 as a daughter house of Savigny in Normandy and was integrated with the Cistercian order in 1147. Dissolved in 1539, part of it was converted into a private mansion. In the 19th century, Neath suffered when the precinct was used for copper smelting and casting. Today the abbey ruins stand as an historic monument.

Shaftesbury Crescent   All that is left of Shaftesbury Abbey in Dorset are ruins and a museum exhibiting a model of the abbey and objects found during excavations of the Benedictine nunnery. In the Middle Ages, the town of Shaftesbury grew up around the nunnery which was endowed by King Alfred in AD 880.

Tintern Close   Tintern Abbey in south-east Wales was the second Cistercian abbey to be founded in Britain in 1131 by Walter de Clare, Lord of Chepstow. Having been added to and updated over the centuries, it was dissolved in 1536. Its beautifully preserved, splendid Gothic ruins have inspired the artist J.M.W. Turner and the poet William Wordsworth.

Torre Close   Torre Abbey near Torquay, Devon was founded as a monastery in 1196. It was later adapted as a country house and in 1741-3 remodelled by the Cary family. In 1930 it was bought by Torbay council and used as an art gallery. There are a few monastic remains.

Westminster Drive   Westminster Abbey, London is an architectural masterpiece of the 13th to 16th centuries. It was founded as a Benedictine monastery over 1,000 years ago. The church was rebuilt by Edward the Confessor in 1065 and again by Henry III in the 13th century in the Gothic style we see today.

Whitby Close   Whitby Abbey, North Yorkshire, an ancient holy place, was once the burial place of kings and an inspiration for saints. A religious community was established at Whitby in AD 657 by Abbess Hilda and was the home of Caedmon, the first English poet. Today's remains, in the care of English Heritage, are of a Benedictine church built in the 13th and 14th centuries, perched high above Whitby harbour.

BARLEYHURST

A small development built in the 1980s and taking the name of a field where barley was grown.

THEME Decisive Battles

Bosworth Close   The Battle of Bosworth Field on 22 August 1485 was fought near Market Bosworth, Leicestershire. Henry Tudor defeated Richard III and thus ended the Wars of the Roses. Richard was killed in the battle and Henry became the first Tudor king, Henry VII.

Normandy Way   Normandy has figured more than once in our history. In 1066,William, Duke of Normandy, led the Norman Conquest of England and became King William I. Almost 900 years later, on 6 June 1944 (D-Day), the Allied Invasion of Normandy was launched from Britain. The battle was long and arduous, but ultimately led to the liberation of France from German occupation and the surrender of Germany in May 1945.

Trafalgar Avenue   A naval battle of the Napoleonic wars, the Battle of Trafalgar was fought on 21 October 1805 off Cape Trafalgar, which lies between Cadiz and Gibraltar. It was the battle in which Nelson in *The Victory* ended the threat of a French invasion of Britain. It was also the battle in which Nelson was killed in his hour of triumph.

Waterloo Court   The Battle of Waterloo was fought on 18 June 1815, outside the small village of Waterloo in central Belgium. It was the battle in which Napoleon Bonaparte was defeated by Dutch, German, Belgian and British forces commanded by Wellington, thus ending the Napoleonic wars. Four days later, Napoleon abdicated, was banished to St Helena and died there in 1821.

THE COUNTIES ESTATE

Cardigan Close   A former county of west Wales, Cardigan in 1974 became part of Dyfed, which also includes Pembrokeshire and Carmarthenshire. Bordering the coast and backed by the Cambrian mountains, Cardigan contains the seaside resort and university town of Aberystwyth. The 7th Earl of Cardigan (1797-1868), who led the Six Hundred into the Valley of Death at Balaklava, also gave his name to the woollen jacket known as a cardigan.

Cheshire Rise   In north-west England, bordering on Wales, Cheshire is mainly a low-lying county at the foot of the Pennines. Dairy farming is its most important industry, particularly the production of the famous Cheshire cheese. Under the local government reorganisation of 1974, Cheshire lost most of its industrial north when Stockport, Merseyside and the Wirral peninsula were transferred to Greater Manchester and Merseyside.

Cork Place   County Cork is the largest county in the Republic of Ireland. Fishing is important off Cork harbour and Bantry Bay. There are several castles, including Blarney, famed for its Blarney Stone. Cork city grew up around a monastery founded there in the sixth century AD.

Cornwall Grove   The most south-westerly county in England and a popular holiday destination, Cornwall's rugged peninsular coastline with its moody, unpredictable seas is notorious for its smugglers' tales and shipwrecks. Inland, gentle fields and valleys contrast with the bleak hills rising to Bodmin Moor. Wherever you go, myths and legends are never far away, and the ruins of Cornwall's tin-mining industry punctuate the landscape.

Cumbria Close   In north-west England, bordering on the Irish Sea, Cumbria was created in 1974 from Cumberland, Westmorland and parts of north-west Lancashire and north-west Yorkshire. It consists of the Lake District, coastal lowlands and the Pennine uplands where sheep farming prevails. On the coast, chemical companies are replacing the old coal, iron and steel industries, while Sellafield (formerly Calder Hall and Windscale atomic energy establishments) is an eerie spectre in a vast and lonely landscape.

Devon Close   In the south-west of England, Devon is renowned for its clotted cream teas, dairy fudge and Honiton lace. With the Atlantic coast on the north side, the English Channel on the south side and sandy beaches on both, Devon is probably the most popular holiday county in England. With the cathedral and university city of Exeter as its capital, large tracts of Exmoor and Dartmoor as well as lush, green fields, Devon's chief industry is both sheep and dairy farming. Its main rivers are the Exe, Dart and Tamar, and Plymouth is a major naval base on the south coast.

Dorset Close   In south-west England between Devon and Hampshire, Dorset borders the English Channel. It consists mainly of lowlands, with the North Dorset Downs and Cranborne Chase in the north and South Dorset Downs near the coast. Livestock farming and tourism, especially around Bournemouth and Weymouth, are its main industries. Thomas Hardy was born at Bockhampton in 1840 and set many of his novels in Dorset, which was his factitious 'Wessex'. He went to school in the county town of Dorchester, which was 'Casterbridge', and, when he died, his body was buried in Westminster Abbey but his heart was buried in the churchyard of the village of Stinsford.

Essex Close   An east of England county bordering Greater London and the North Sea coast, where Harwich is a major ferry port and oyster beds are cultivated in the Colne estuary. Colchester, founded in AD 10 by Cymbeline, was an important Roman capital with Roman walls still visible in the town today. A flat county, the fields of Essex grow sugar beet, potatoes and other vegetables.

Glamorgan Close   A former county of South Wales bordering the Bristol Channel, Glamorgan was divided into Mid, East and West Glamorgan and Gwent under local government reorganisation in 1974. The area includes the Vale of Neath and the Rhondda, the Gower Peninsula, Swansea, Cardiff and Caerphilly, where the cheese comes from.

Hampshire Court   In southern England, Hampshire borders the English Channel at Southampton, Gosport and Portsmouth. Inland, it has gentle, undulating lowlands and chalk downlands in the north and east of the county.

Hertford Place   Hertford is the county town of Hertfordshire, a home county to the north of London. Urbanised on the London border around Barnet and Watford, east and west Hertfordshire retains its rural beauty, with open fields, woodland and arable and dairy farming. Its industries include flour milling, brewing and printing.

Middlesex Drive   The historic county of Middlesex, with its several market towns, was absorbed by Greater London in 1965, when Staines and Sunbury were given to Surrey and Potters Bar to Hertfordshire. Other Middlesex towns included Brentford, where the Grand Union canal meets the river Thames, Harrow on the Hill above the Middlesex plain, Enfield and Uxbridge.

Nottingham Grove   Nottingham is the county town of Nottinghamshire in the East Midlands. With the river Trent running through it, the county is renowned for Robin Hood, who lived in Sherwood Forest, D.H. Lawrence, who was born at Eastwood and set his novels in the grimy coalfields which once blackened the north of the county, and for Nottinghamshire lace, traditionally made in the south of the county. It was at Nottingham that Charles I raised his standard in 1642 at the outbreak of the Civil War.

Shropshire Court   In the West Midlands and bordering Wales, the Shropshire lowlands and uplands are separated by the river Severn. This was the main iron-producing county in the 18th century and the first cast-iron bridge in the world was built at Ironbridge in 1779. The county was immortalised by the poet A.E. Housman (1859-1936) in his ballad, *A Shropshire Lad*. Shrewsbury, with its boys' public school, is the county town.

Somerset Close   In south-west England and bordering the Bristol Channel, Somerset includes the Quantock hills and Exmoor in the west and the Blackdown and Mendip hills (famous for Cheddar and Wookey Hole caves) in the north east. The county town is Taunton and dairy farming and cider are its main industries.

Suffolk Close   An eastern county, sandwiched between Essex and Norfolk and bordering the North Sea, Suffolk is largely agricultural lowland growing cereals and sugar beet. Cardinal Wolsey was born in Ipswich, which is the county town. Benjamin Britten was born at Lowestoft, established the Aldeburgh Festival in 1948, set his opera *Peter Grimes* in the town and was knighted Baron Britten of Aldeburgh in 1976. John Constable was born at East Bergholt on the river Stour and his paintings are a record of Suffolk's timeless beauty.

Surrey Road   One of the home counties in south-east England, and bordering Greater London, Surrey is mainly a residential county in the commuter belt, but also has pockets of peace and beauty in its heaths, commons and woodlands, as at Wimbledon, Virginia Water, Bagshot, Kew and Wisley. The North Downs run east to west across the middle of the county. The historic county town of Guildford and the old wool town of Godalming bear testimony to Surrey's past, while Kingston-upon-Thames is its modern administrative centre.

Sussex Road   Since 1974, this county has been divided into East and West Sussex. On the south coast, it contains the resorts of Eastbourne, Brighton, Worthing and Bognor Regis, and historic towns of Hastings, Arundel and Chichester, with its harbour and ancient cathedral. Inland, the South Downs roll over to meet the Weald.

Waterford Close   A county of the Republic of Ireland (Eire), Waterford is famous for its crystal. A hilly region with the rivers Blackwater and Suir running through it, cattle rearing and dairy farming are its main industries. Waterford city is an important port, trading and distribution centre.

Wiltshire Way   A swathe of southern England between Somerset and the Berkshire Downs, Wiltshire's history and evocative charm lies mainly across Salisbury Plain. Its rolling fields are crossed by ancient paths trodden by Bronze-Age men on their way to Avebury Stone Circle or Stonehenge. Salisbury Cathedral contains some of the stones from the Roman fortress of Old Sarum, the foundations of which are nearby. Swindon is an important railway town and Trowbridge is the administrative centre.

THE SCOTTS ESTATE

Aberdeen Close   Scotland's third largest city, Aberdeen is on the North Sea coast and is the administrative centre of the Grampian region. The city, on the rivers Don and Dee, is built almost entirely of locally quarried granite, which also provided the cobbles for many London streets in the 18th century. Aberdeen has always been an important fishing port, and with the discovery of North Sea oil it became an important service centre for the oil industry. The Aberdeen area, a county until 1975, is famed for its Aberdeen Angus beef cattle.

Angus Drive   A Scottish Highland county on the east coast whose towns include Montrose and Dundee. The coast has alternating sandy beeches and steep cliffs, sweeping bays and salt flats. The vale of Strathmore lies at the heart of Angus and divides the Grampians from the Sidlaw hills. The county is famed for its Aberdeen Angus cattle and Dundee cake.

Arbroath Close   Arbroath is a fishing port, famous for 'smokies', haddock browned and flavoured by the smoke of an oak fire. Scotland's Declaration of Independence was signed in 1320 at Arbroath Abbey, which is now a ruin. The stone of Scone, the coronation stone of Britain, was discovered hidden under the high altar in 1951 after it had been stolen from Westminster Abbey.

Ayr Way   Ayr is the county town of Ayrshire on the west coast. The area is famed for its white and brown Ayrshire dairy cows and early potatoes. Ayr town is a resort with good beaches, a fishing harbour and connections with Robert Burns, who was born two miles away at Alloway. The Brig o' Doon in his poem *Tam O' Shanter* still spans the river. It is a simple, arched bridge.

Berwick Drive   The border town of Berwick-on-Tweed lies on the northernmost tip of Northumberland and its ownership has long been disputed between England and Scotland. Once a great Scottish port, it changed hands 14 times before becoming English in the 14th century. Berwickshire, however, is a Scottish county and North Berwick is on the coast of the Firth or Forth, looking out to the Bass Rock nature reserve which is famous for its gannets.

Bute Brae   Bute is an island 15 miles long at the foot of the Cowal peninsula, from which it is separated by the Kyles of Bute. The island is hilly to the north and flat in the south. Rothesay is the main town, resort and steamer port. A brae is a hilly slope bounding a riverside plain.

Caithness Court   Caithness, on the north-eastern tip of the Scottish Highlands, has Wick, an important herring-fishing port, as its main town and Thurso, a fishing resort looking across to the Orkneys. The mountainous seas create breathtaking seascapes, and many wrecks lie on the rocks at the foot of the cliffs. Parts of inland Caithness are flat, uninhabited and treeless. On this surface-of-the-moon landscape stands the Dounreay atomic reactor. Caithness is famed for its fine cut glass made at the glassworks near Wick.

Coldharbour Church of England Combined School   Coldharbour, meaning a cold settlement, was the name of this area to the north of Bletchley and Coldharbour Farm stood roughly where the school now stands.

Cromarty Court   Cromarty in the north-east Highlands is sandwiched between Sutherland and Inverness. Ullapool is the main town and on the rugged west coast there are sheltered glens and the land, warmed by the gulf stream, is unexpectedly green. At Poolewe a collection of sub-tropical plants survives in the gardens of Inverewe.

Dumfries Close   Dumfriesshire has a turbulent and romantic history of fierce battles and feuds which have inspired many songs and ballads, including *Annie Laurie*. The town of Dumfries on the banks of the river Nith is where Robert Burns lived from 1791 until his death in 1796, and where he wrote *Auld Lang Syne* and *Ye Banks and Braes of Bonnie Doon*.

Forfar Drive   Forfar, in east Scotland, was the county town of Angus until 1975 when, under local government reorganisation, it became part of Tayside Region. Lying in the vale of Strathmore, Forfar is a few miles from Glamis castle, the ancestral home of the Strathmore family and the late Queen Elizabeth the Queen Mother.

Galloway Close   Galloway, in the west of the Scottish Southern Uplands, is best known for the wild and beautiful slopes of the mountains, with southern Scotland's highest peak, Merrick, rising to 2,766 feet. It is an area containing Kirkcudbrightshire and Wigtonshire and is famous for black, hornless Galloway cattle and red deer, wild goats and the golden eagle.

Haddington Close   Haddington is the county town of East Lothian. The town was laid out in the 12th century as a long, narrow triangle and has several buildings of special architectural interest. East Lothian is Scotland's main agricultural region.

Highland Close   The Highlands of Scotland can be described roughly as the northern half of the country. They cover about a quarter of Britain's land surface, but fewer than one in fifty of the population live there. Wild, rugged and lonely, the Highlands bear many traces of human occupation, with crumbling crofts and ruined castles set in spectacular scenery with abundant wildlife.

Inverness Close   Inverness is the capital city of the Highland Region of Scotland. Lying at the head of the Moray Firth, it is a tourist centre with a 19th-century cathedral and a castle built to replace an earlier one destroyed in 1746. Boat-building, iron founding, woollens and distilling are among its industries.

Kincardine Drive   In Fife, on the river Forth, Kincardine has a major road bridge carrying the A876 across the river from the M9. Before the building of the Forth Road Bridge, this was the lowest road bridging-point of the river.

Kinross Drive   Kinross, the county town of Kinross-shire, stands on Loch Leven which is famed for its salmon-trout. When the loch freezes in winter it is used for the sport of curling. In the middle of the loch stand the ruins of a 15th-century castle from which Mary Queen of Scots escaped in 1568.

Lothian Close   East, West and Midlothian are the areas around Edinburgh. West Lothian, once an agricultural area, was spoiled by the 19th-century oil-shale industry which scarred the landscape with its shale heaps. About half of Midlothian falls within the urban area of Edinburgh, with the Pentland and Moorfoot hills rising in the other half. East Lothian lies between the Lammermuir Hills and the coast and has some of Scotland's finest agricultural land as well as a fishing industry. The area is also renowned for its golf courses.

Moray Place   A small county in the Highlands, Moray is bordered by Banff,

Nairn, Inverness and the Moray Firth. It is a rich farming area with fishing villages on the coast, which is known as the Scottish riviera, because of its beaches rather than its heat! Elgin, with its ruined 18th-century cathedral, is Moray's tourist centre.

Nairn Court   Nairn, a small town on the Moray Firth, north Scotland, has a long history as a fishing port, but since Victorian times it has also been a popular holiday resort. On its inland side there is beautiful woodland countryside and four castles to visit. Cawdor castle, built in the 14th century, is still home to the Cawdor family.

Orkney Close   The Orkney Islands lie to the north-east of the Scottish mainland. Of the 65 islands, only 30 are inhabited. In the ninth century, Norsemen settled in the Orkneys and for 500 years they were ruled by Norway or Denmark. They became Scottish in about 1468, when Christian I pawned them in lieu of a dowry on his daughter's marriage to James III of Scotland. The Orkneys are rich in scenery, wildlife and history.

Peebles Place   A county town on the river Tweed, Peebles is a tweed and knitwear manufacturing town as well as a salmon fishing centre. A 15th-century bridge crosses the river. In 1800 and 1802 William and Robert Chamber, who established *Chambers Dictionary*, were born here.

Perth Close   Known as 'the Fair City', Perth was once the capital of Scotland, having been made so by James VI of Scotland (who became James I of England). In 1437 it was the scene of the assassination of James I of Scotland. Today it has carpet, textiles, dyeing and whisky distilling industries. The former county of Perth was described by Sir Walter Scott in his novel *The Fair Maid of Perth* as the most beautiful and varied of all the counties in Scotland.

Renfrew Way   A small Scottish county west of Glasgow, Renfrew borders the Clyde and the Firth of Clyde. Its towns include Greenock, birthplace in 1736 of James Watt, inventor of the steam engine, and once an industrial and shipbuilding centre. Paisley was the largest thread manufacturing centre in the world and is famous for its shawls and cloth patterns.

Ross Way   Ross and Cromarty have been 'married' for years. Together they formed a county of north Scotland until, following local government reorganisation in 1975, boundaries were altered and Ross and Cromarty became a district within the Highland Region.

Roxburgh Way   Roxburgh is one of Scotland's Border counties, separated from England by the Cheviot hills. Its violent history of bandits and battles against the English between the 13th and 17th centuries is evidenced by the ruins of the county's four great abbeys at Melrose, Jedburgh, Kelso and Dryburgh. It inspired the writings of Sir Walter Scott, who lived at Abbotsford.

Selkirk Grove   Selkirk is a Border town with a history of shoemaking and tweed manufacture, made possible by the many rivers which flow into the Tweed and the sheep farming which provides the wool for the cloth. The explorer Mungo Park (1771-1806) lived here and there is a statue of him in the High Street.

Sutherland Grove   The Scottish county of Sutherland is a great expanse of wild land that stretches out towards Cape Wrath. In the 19th century it suffered terribly during the Highland Clearances, when thousands of people were driven from the land by the landowners to make way for sheep and deer. As a result of burning, the land never recovered and it is one of the least populated areas in Britain, with thousands of acres of spectacular wilderness.

CALDECOTTE

A common place-name, particularly in south-east and central England, several Caldecotes lie close to Roman roads or tracks. From Old English cald *and* cot, *the name means 'cold or inhospitable cottages or shelter for travellers'. This Caldecotte, beside the river Ouzel and a short distance from Watling Street and the site of the Roman city of Magiovinium, was a small hamlet and farming area attached to Bow Brickhill. Domesday Book records that it had a valuable Saxon watermill which was worth ten shillings a year, but the Milton Keynes Heritage map, published in 1983 by the Development Corporation, identifies 11 historic sites in this south-east corner of Milton Keynes. Apart from the watermill, which was excavated in 1980, there was an Iron-Age religious site, a Roman settlement with early pottery kilns, a Saxon settlement, excavated in 1972, a medieval village, earthworks and moat, and two farmhouses of 1600 and 1850. Caldecotte Brickyard, dated about 1750, was excavated in 1980 and in 1982 excavations unearthed the remains of a boat, dated about 1700, and a fossilised Icthyosaurus (a gigantic fish-like reptile). Despite the fact that Milton Keynes Development Corporation in 1971 listed Caldecotte Farmhouse, 17th-century timber-framed and thatched, and all that remained on the site of the Medieval Shrunken Village as worthy of preservation, it seems to have been destroyed.*

THEMES **(1) The Parish History of Bow Brickhill and Walton (2) Watermills**

Backleys   'Back Leys' was the name of an 11-acre field shown on the 1791 Caldecotte enclosure map as belonging to Anne Parker.

Berrystead   'Berrystead Close' was the name of a field shown on a Survey and

Plan of the Lordship of Bow Brickhill of 1791, when the field was divided and enclosed, and 'Jos Ager Esquire exchanged with Charlotte Primatt'.

Brantham Close   Brantham, on the river Stour in Suffolk, once had a medieval tide mill which depended on both salt water taken from the sea and fresh water from the river.

Caldecotte Lake Drive   This leads from the main road, Brickhill Street, down to Caldecotte lake and the business park.

Caldecotte Lane   This is the remains of an old lane which led off Walton Road to the hamlet of Caldecotte.

Gatewick Lane   In the 15th century, Gatewick Mill in Sussex was one of two watermills belonging to Charlton Manor. It later belonged to Gatewick Manor and was demolished in 1878.

Hele Court   At Hele, on the north Devon coast next to Ilfracombe, there is a 16th-century watermill which has been restored to working order. Dating from 1525, it has an 18ft overshot wheel and produces wholemeal stoneground flour and muesli. Above the village is a 447ft-high Iron-Age hillfort. In 1086, Hele was held by Drogo for Geoffrey, Bishop of Coutances, who also held the lands and watermills of Simpson and Water Eaton.

Heybridge Crescent   Heybridge Mill on the river Chelmer, east of Maldon in Essex, was a working mill until 1942, but was demolished in 1955 although the mill house remains. Near by, Heybridge Basin, which once accommodated large ships carrying coal from Newcastle and timber from Scandinavia, now provides water sports facilities and a sailing club, similar to Caldecotte lake.

Home Field   This was the name of a field.

Langford Place   In 1776, Langford Mill at the confluence of the rivers Chelmer and Blackwater in Essex was a weather-boarded mill, operated by both steam and water power. After it burned down in 1876, it was rebuilt of brick and continued as a milling business until the First World War. It was then bought by Essex Water Company, who installed a water extraction pump. The mill race now forms a reservoir for supplying water to the Chelmer and Blackwater Canal.

Long Ayres   The name of a field formerly owned by the Dickins family.

Longhedge   This refers to 'Long Hedge Ground', the name of a 10-acre field listed on the Caldecotte enclosure map of 1791 as one of 10 fields then owned by Anne Parker.

Maple Durham   The small village of Mapledurham, on the river Thames near Reading, has a medieval watermill which has been restored to working order, with the original 15th-century roof and wall timbers still intact. There is boating on the river and Mapledurham House, an Elizabethan mansion owned by the Blount family, has been featured in versions of

John Galsworthy's *The Forsyte Saga*, and Kenneth Grahame's *Wind in the Willows*.

Martel Close   The Martel family were lords of the manor of Tattenhoe after it was granted to Ralph Martel by King John. Ralph Martel was the founder of Snelshall Priory for Benedictine monks at some time between 1203-19. It is said that the little church of St Giles, Tattenhoe was built from the stones of the priory ruins. Margaret, wife of Geoffrey Martel, inherited land in Bow Brickhill from her father, Stephen de Thurnham, upon his death in 1216.

Monellan Grove and Monellan Crescent   The Delaps of Monellan acquired Bow Brickhill at the beginning of the 19th century, through the marriage of James Bogle Delap to Harriett Hillier. She was the daughter of Nathaniel Hillier, landowner in Bow Brickhill and Caldecotte in 1793. Lt Col James Bogle Delap still owned Bow Brickhill Manor in 1847, and his widow in 1854.

Mortain Close   Domesday landowner Robert, Count of Mortain was half-brother of William the Conqueror and younger brother of Odo of Bayeux. He married the daughter of Earl Hugh of Chester, was virtual Earl of Cornwall, Lord of the Sussex rape (division) of Pevensey and its castle, and his fief (lands held for a fee on condition of military service) included the Honour of Berkhamsted and its castle. After the King, Mortain was the largest landholder in the country, with holdings in 19 counties. In Buckinghamshire he held parts of Loughton, Woughton and Mursley as well as Caldecotte, Bow Brickhill and Wavendon. In 1088 he rebelled but was pardoned and died in 1091.

The Caldecotte Arms *hotel, appropriately designed to replicate an old mill, beside Caldecotte lake. The windmill was constructed with authentic parts imported from Holland.*

Newark Court   This takes the name of Newark Mill, which stood on the river Wey near Ripley in Surrey. Recorded in Domesday Book, it was later gifted to Newark Priory by the Sande family. The mill was rebuilt sometime around the 1650s and was later extended, with a third waterwheel made of metal added in the 1850s. When machine-operated mills replaced water power after 1930, Newark Mill produced animal feeds. After the cogs were damaged in 1943 it remained idle, and was destroyed by a fire in 1963.

Onslow Court   The Hon. Thomas Cranley Onslow married Susan Eliza Hillier, daughter of Nathaniel Hillier of Stoke Park, who owned lands in Caldecotte in 1793. Susan's sister Harriett married James Bogle Delap. (See Monellan Grove and Crescent.)

The Nortons   This name groups together four adjoining fields at Caldecotte – Nortons north meadow, Nortons middle meadow, Nortons south meadow and Nortons close – totalling about 40 acres.

Top Meadow   This was the name of a field owned by the Dickins family, local landowners, who contributed 300 acres of land for the building of the new city of Milton Keynes.

Tredington Grove   This refers to Tredington Mill in Warwickshire.

Walton Road   A short section of the old road which ran from Bow Brickhill to Walton.

FENNY STRATFORD

Although described in Magna Britannia *in 1806 as a 'small, decayed market town', Fenny Stratford was once more prosperous than Bletchley. On the Roman Watling Street, it was strategically placed for the travelling trade and had several coaching inns. It also benefited from the building of the Grand Junction (now Grand Union) canal, on which it stands, and was a busy little town in its own right until the railways came, Bletchley grew, and Fenny Stratford wilted in its shadow. The name comes from the Old English* straet *and* ford, *meaning 'ford on a Roman road', the affix* fennig *meaning 'marshy'.*

THEME History of the Parish

Aylesbury Street   Robert Stephenson decided that the new railway line in 1831 should run from Aylesbury, through Fenny Stratford, to Stony Stratford and Castlethorpe because of the suitability of the low-lying land.

Baisley House   James Baisley, a hay and corn merchant, was one of the first 12 members of Fenny Stratford Urban District Council when it was

Fenny Stratford main street, c.1819, from a print engraved by J. Hassell.

instigated in 1895. Elected its first Chairman, he served in that office until 1900 but continued as a Councillor for 20 years.

Belvedere Lane   The name Belvedere comes from Old French *bel* and *vedeir* which, by 1130, became *belveder*, meaning 'beautiful view'. The lane leads to Belvedere farm which is on the fringe of the site of Magiovinium, a Romano-British settlement where pottery has been found as well as evidence of an encampment with ditched enclosures and a cemetery with cremated remains. Speculation that there may also have been a small fort has yet to be proved.

Bristow Close   This refers to J.P. Bristow of the London Brick Company, which acquired Bletchley Brick Company in 1929.

Browne Willis Close   Browne Willis was a well-known 18th-century antiquarian and local benefactor. Lord of the manor of Fenny Stratford, he lived at Whaddon Hall and was a devout churchman. He built St Martin's church, Fenny Stratford and was buried there in 1760. By his generosity, several other local churches were restored including those of Bletchley, Bow and Little Brickhill and the tower of St Mary Magdalen, Stony Stratford after the rest of the church was destroyed by fire in 1742.

Bull Lane   This is where the *Bull Inn* stands. It is one of the oldest inns in Fenny Stratford.

Church Street   St Martin's church stands here, a listed building with dates ranging from 1730 to 1907. The foundation stone was laid by well-known antiquarian Browne Willis in 1724 on St Martin's Day, and he dedicated it to St Martin because his grandfather died on St Martin's Day in St Martin's Lane, London.

Denmark Street   Probably named after Edward VII's queen, Alexandra of Denmark.

Durrans Court   Mr Durran was an optician in Fenny Stratford during the 1920s-30s. He had a practice on the corner of Watling Street and Aylesbury Street, almost on the site of Durrans Court, and is still remembered as living with his matriarchal mother, who 'dressed like a Duchess' in silver fox furs.

Fenny Lock   With a slip road onto the new A5 trunk road on one side and the Grand Union canal on the other, this is the site of a Tesco distribution centre. Lock number 22, Fenny Lock and pumphouse, is at the start of the canal's long climb southwards through a series of locks to Tring Summit. It is the shallowest lock on the Grand Union and the only one with a swing-bridge across the lock chamber. At this point it is crossed by the Bletchley to Bedford branch railway line.

George Street   Named after King George V who visited the area in 1911. 'George V' was also a class of locomotive, a big passenger tender engine based at Bletchley in 1917.

Hawthorn Avenue   On the Trees Estate, which links Fenny Stratford to Water Eaton, hawthorn is a small tree or shrub of the rose family, usually grown to form hedgerows.

Laburnum Grove   The laburnum is a small tree often grown in gardens for its drooping yellow flowers in May and June. Its seed pods are notoriously poisonous.

Lock View Lane   This lane leads to the canal at Fenny Lock number 22, and the pumphouse.

Manor Fields   Now playing fields, this is where the manor once stood. The manor of Fenny Stratford was held jointly with Water Eaton by Roger de

Fenny Stratford lock, on the Grand Union canal in the south of the city, lowers the canal by only 13 inches, making it the shallowest lock on the Grand Union.

Caux in 1204 and John Grey in 1252. The de Greys, Dukes of Buckingham, sold it in the 17th century to a London physician, Thomas Willis, whose grandson, Browne Willis, inherited in about 1800.

Manor Road   Once called Water Eaton Lane and winding between hedgerows on its way from Fenny to Water Eaton, this was re-named Manor Road because it skirts the area known as Manor Fields, where the ancient manor of Fenny Stratford once stood, and the Water Hall manor of Eaton, which stood by the river Ouzel in Saffron Gardens Park. The late 17th-/early 18th-century building, Manor Farm, still bears the name.

Maple Grove   Maple trees belong to the acer family. Maple syrup is made from the sap of some species.

Napier Street   D. Napier & Son was an engineering firm which, in the 1950s, was a subsidiary of English Electric. At a time when steam was being replaced by diesel, English Electric produced an extremely powerful engine of 1,650 horsepower which they named the Napier Deltic. Two of these engines were used to power the 'Deltic' locomotive.

Oakwood Drive   The oak is a venerable tree, particularly revered by the English, with many legends attached to it. Historically used as a building material and in shipbuilding, its strong, hard timber is exceptionally durable. The tree's longevity means there are several famous oaks in the region, including 'The Abbot's Oak' near Woburn Abbey, from a branch of which the Abbot of Woburn was hanged in 1537 by order of Henry VIII.

Paddock Way   The paddock was a piece of land behind the *Bull Inn*. The original 'Fenny Poppers' (a battery of six guns) were fired here for the last time in 1856, when a splinter of fire landed on the roof of the *Bull and Butcher* inn and partially destroyed it.

Penn Road   Probably named after William Penn, the ardent 17th-century Quaker who founded Pennsylvania. The Quakers established a Friendly

Fenny Stratford n Watling Street, in front of the Navigation Inn.

In Fenny Stratford and dating from 1495, this was the Guildhall, hospital and chantry of the Guild of St Margaret and St Katherine the Virgins, founded in 1493. The building became Holdom's Brewery in 1880 and the factory premises of Valentin Ord and Nagle, sugar brewers, c.1910.

Society in Fenny Stratford and held their meetings at *The Crown* in the High Street from 1794 until 1800, when they moved to the *Swan Inn*. Relatives of William Penn owned a tanners yard in Stony Stratford during the 17th century.

Pinewood Drive   Pine woods are a characteristic feature of the area, particularly on the hillsides of nearby Bow Brickhill and Woburn.

Rhondda Close   Named in memory of Rhondda House, home of the Rowland family, timber merchants (see Rowlands Close). This stood close to Staple Hall and was owned by Thomas Evans Rowland in the 19th century. *Kelly's Directory* records Mrs Rowland living there by 1931.

Rowlands Close   Thomas Evans Rowland and William Richard Rowland were brothers who established a timber business in 1874 with their sawmill and timber yard beside the canal off Simpson Road. They sold the business in 1942 to James Latham and Company, who still own it.

Saffron Gardens   Now a local park, this land by the river Ouzel was once covered with saffron, a species of crocus the dried stigmas from which were used as an orange-yellow dye and a flavouring agent.

Saracens Wharf   On the canal, the wharf was once a private dock with a swing-bridge across it. An old inn close by on Watling Street was once well known as *The Saracens Head*. Also, the *Saracen* was a railway engine of the 'Experiment' class, located at Bletchley from about 1912-18.

Simpson Road   This is the road leading to Simpson.

Staplehall Road   Staple Hall is shown on an Ordnance Survey map of 1889 as an area of Fenny Stratford. A mansion named Staple Hall stood on this

Staple Hall, Fenny Stratford with men of the Royal Engineers, stationed here during the First World War.

site, and during the First World War it was occupied by the Royal Engineers when large numbers of troops were undergoing training in Bletchley.

Stratford Marina   Stratford, meaning a ford on a Roman road, and Marina, a mooring for pleasure craft beside the canal. This is now a housing development.

Stuart Close   In the early 19th century, Charles Stuart took over an ironworks in Denmark Street. His son, Herbert Ackroyd Stuart (1864-1927), renowned at the time for carrying out 'explosive' experiments, developed and produced an oil-fuelled compression engine which was patented two years before Rudolf Diesel was credited with having invented the first compression ignition engine. About eight of Ackroyd Stuart's engines were made in Bletchley before he sold the patent to Richard Hornsby & Sons of Grantham.

Sycamore Avenue   Sycamore trees are of the acer family and similar to, although larger than, the maple. Sycamore Farm House, close by in Drayton Road, Water Eaton, is a listed 18th-century building which may well have suggested the naming of this Trees Estate.

The Beeches   There were probably beech trees growing here.

The Laurels   There were probably laurel bushes growing here.

Canal Bridge House, on Watling Street, was built in the 19th century for brickmaker Gregory Odell Clarke. A listed building, it is sadly being allowed to become dilapidated.

The Limes   Limes are graceful, spreading trees with grey bark and heart-shaped leaves. The pollen of their yellowish, scented flowers is very attractive to bees in July.

Vicarage Road   The road where the Vicarage to St Martin's church stands.

Victoria Road   Named after Queen Victoria.

Walnut Drive   Before the Industrial Revolution, the expansion of Bletchley and, latterly, the building of Milton Keynes, trees were a major feature of the north Buckinghamshire countryside. Walnut trees were extensively grown and cultivated for their nuts, particularly in this area of Bletchley and around Wavendon. The 17th-century Walnut Tree Cottage in Church Green Road, Bletchley bears witness to this.

Watling Terrace   This is a terrace off Watling Street, which dates from the late ninth century when it was called *Waeclinga straet,* meaning a Roman road associated with the family name 'Wacol'.

Wharfside   This is a wharf by the side of the canal.

SIMPSON

Simpson is one of the original 13 villages incorporated in the new city of Milton Keynes. Recorded in Domesday Book 1086 as Siwinestone, the name derives from a man named Sigewine, who had a farmstead there in Anglo-Saxon days. Closely related throughout history to its neighbour, Fenny Stratford, Simpson was described in the 1830s as 'one of the most wretched of many miserable villages in the county', mainly because, during winter, a 200-yard stretch of the road through the village was impassable due to flood water lying three feet deep. Through the parish flows the river Ouzel, beside which are the sites of a medieval moat and fishponds and a 16th-century manor.

THEME **The History of the Parish**

Abbey Road   Although Geoffrey, Bishop of Coutances was lord of the manor from 1075-9, there is no evidence of there ever having been an abbey in Simpson. However, according to Domesday Book, the monks of St Pierre de la Couture held five hides in the manor of neighbouring Great Woolstone until about 1243. The nearest monasteries were Newton Longville Priory and Tickford Abbey, both founded in the early 12th century.

Chandler Court   Named after John Chandler, a bell founder who made the bells for several local churches, including No. 2 bell for Simpson church in 1694. The Chandler family lived at Drayton Parslow. Richard Chandler made three bells for the church of St Mary Magdalene at Willen in 1683 and the first bell for St Lawrence, Bradwell in 1700. Anthony Chandler made one for St Michael's church at Walton in 1709.

Hanmer Road   In the 18th century, Job Hanmer (1677-1738) married Susanna Walden, daughter and heiress of the lord of the manor, and thereby the Simpson estate passed to the Hanmer family. Their son, Sir Walden Hanmer, was largely responsible for the construction of the old Groveway road in about 1770. Thomas Walden Hanmer was rector of the parish church of St Thomas the Apostle in 1807. There are several monuments to the Hanmers in the church, including one by the 18th-century sculptor John Bacon.

Lissel Road   Lissel is a variant of the river name Ouzel.

Millholm Rise   There was an Anglo-Saxon watermill at Simpson. The Old English word *holm* means an island in a river, raised ground in a marsh or a river meadow, so this name seems to refer to the old mill which would have been somewhere near the river here.

Mount Pleasant   A pleasant place on a hill or mount.

Old Groveway   This is a section of the old road which has been called Groveway since at least the 18th century.

Poplar Close   The Poplars is the name of an early 19th-century house.

Simpson and Simpson Drive   These are access roads into Simpson village from the main Groveway grid-road.

Simpson Road   This is the original road between Simpson and Fenny Stratford.

The Mount   A close of dwellings built on the brow of the hill which falls down to the village. Mount is the Middle English word for a hill.

The church tower behind the preserved footings of the Manor House, Simpson.

The river Ouse in flood in the 1970s.

Walton Road   This is a section of the old road which led from Simpson to Walton village and now comes to a dead end.

Warren Bank   This takes its name from a piece of land which was known as 'The Warren'. A warren, most commonly thought of as a colony of rabbits, also means a piece of ground kept for breeding game, especially hares, rabbits and partridge, and the right to keep and hunt this game. In 1243, Sir John Grey, lord of Simpson and several other manors, and Sheriff of Buckinghamshire and Bedfordshire, secured his family's right to 'free warren in all his demesne lands including (Water) Eton and Bletchley'. Also, Charles Warren in the early 1860s led a successful campaign to improve the road through the village. He built a fine villa here with gardens containing grottoes, summer-houses, rockeries, fountains and fishponds. The house is now known as Simpson House and was renovated in the early 1970s.

TILBROOK

Named after Tilbrook Farm at Bow Brickhill, this industrial area is built on land adjacent to the Bletchley to Bedford branch railway line. Among the variety of companies operating here is Red Bull Racing, which in 2005 bought out Jaguar Racing Ltd, which had operated here for many years.

Bradbourne Drive   The Bradbourne river is a tributary of the river Derwent.

Sherbourne Drive   The Sherbourne is another tributary of the Derwent.

WATER EATON

The border between Water Eaton and Fenny Stratford, two areas of Bletchley conjoined through their combined manorial past, was obliterated with the building of the Trees Estate shortly after the Second World War to provide urgently needed housing. Sadly, the theme may have been chosen because of the number of trees cut down to facilitate this development. Today, Water Eaton brook is all that separates Water Eaton from Fenny Stratford but Water Eaton has several old cottages and farmhouses bearing witness to its agricultural past. In the mid-19th century, and up until about 1925, there were five large farms, about 40 cottages and a thriving farming community.

THEMES **Local History and Flora**

Appleby Heath   Believed to have been named after Herbert Appleby, who for many years was works foreman at Flettons Brick Works. Flettons Ltd opened at Skew Bridge, Bletchley in 1929 and operated several local brick fields, including one at Water Eaton. They were taken over by London Brick Company in 1950.

Baccara Grove   On what is known as the 'Roses' estate, the Black Baccara is a black rose with velvety petals of a deep colour, a strong scent and long-lasting blooms.

Barton Road   It has been suggested that this road was named after William Barton, a teacher in 1388, and the Barton family who endowed a free grammar school at Thornton in the 15th century. However, a more likely candidate seems to be the Reverend Philip Barton, rector of Great Brickhill, who in about 1767 acquired the manors of Bletchley and Water Eaton and, two years later, also inherited the manor of Great Brickhill. When he died in 1786 without children, he left his estates to his godson, Philip Duncombe Pauncefoot, a baby at the time, on condition that he assumed the name Duncombe. The Barton family were also lords of the manor of Stoke Hammond at that time.

Bettina Grove   On the estate known as the 'Roses', Elizabeth von Arnim (1785-1859) was a German writer and wife of poet Ludwig Achim von Arnim. Her first book, *Letters to a Child* (1835), was based on her letters to Goethe. The Bettina rose named after her is a climbing hybrid tea rose of a coppery-orange to peach-buff colour.

Bishop Parker RC Combined School is named after Monsignor Leo Parker, Bishop of the Catholic Diocese of Northampton during the 1940-50s.

Celina Close   Celina is a moss rose with heavily massed buds which open into dark crimson flowers sometimes streaked with white.

Chestnut Crescent   On the Trees Estate. The sweet chestnut is a spreading tree with a smooth, grey bark and edible chestnuts wrapped in a soft, spiny case, while the horse chestnut has a grey bark, white flowers growing upwards like candles and hard brown nuts, or 'conkers', wrapped in a softer, spikey case.

Cornelia Close   Cornelia, the model of Roman matronly virtue, has given her name to a hybrid musk rose which has fragrant flowers of flushed, strawberry pink and bronze foliage. Although blooming through the summer, Cornelia improves in the autumn.

Doreen Close   A variety of rose named 'Doreen' no doubt existed at the time this road was named, but no trace has been found of it. The only rose today bearing the name is the Mrs Doreen Pike, an English shrub rose bred by David Austin in 1993. It has pink, very fragrant double blooms which usually flower twice during the summer.

Drayton Road   Leading out from the village centre, this road goes to the nearby village of Drayton Parslow.

Eaton Leys   This is a large expanse of water meadow on the far side of the Ouzel. Eaton Leys farm in the 1850s covered 183 acres for which the rent was £1 10s. per acre.

Eaton Mill Combined School takes its name from the mill beside the river Ouzel.

Frensham Drive   The Frensham is a floribunda rose. With bright red flowers, it is very thorny, grows vigorously and is often used as a hedging rose.

Harkness Close   Harkness is the well-known name of a family of rose growers. Some of their roses bear the family name, as in Elizabeth Harkness, a bush rose with large flowers and profuse, dark green foliage, and Rosemary Harkness, a bush rose with scented blooms in shades of salmon pink.

Hazel Grove   The hazel is a tall shrub with a reddish-brown bark, pale-yellow catkins in early spring and nuts encased in a leafy shell.

Hunter Drive   The de Greys, who were lords of most of the manors around Bletchley for 400 years, were great huntsmen. In the Middle Ages, there was a deer park and another park 'of great trees' covering 20 acres at Water Eaton. In 1324, Lord Grey de Ruthin held the manor of Eatone, as it was then called, in return for keeping a falcon for flight for the king's use, generally providing the king with the equipment for a good day's hunting and entertaining him.

Larch Grove   A continuation of the Trees Estate. The larch is a deciduous variety of fir tree. No. 8 Larch Grove is a listed 17th-century, white, thatched cottage.

Seventeenth-century cottages in Mill Road, Water Eaton.

Magenta Close   The Magenta Floorshow rose has large, scented double blooms of a rich, deep reddish-purple colour.

Mill Road   There are several 17th- to 19th-century white, thatched cottages in Mill Road, which leads to the old mill. There has been a mill on the river at Water Eaton since at least Saxon times and it is mentioned in Domesday Book as being worth 20 shillings a year, one of the most valuable mills on the Ouzel. It is now disused and the millrace has been diverted. The present 19th-century mill house was a farm for many years and is now a private house.

Saffron Street   As in Saffron Gardens, Fenny Stratford, this recalls the medieval past when yellow crocuses were cultivated in the riverside meadows for the production of saffron.

Stoke Road   Leading off what was once the green at the centre of the village and is now a conglomeration of mini roundabouts, this is the main road to the nearby village of Stoke Hammond.

The Wharf   The wharf beside the Grand Union canal, with its group of 19th-century canal houses, was operated in the 1860s by Gregory Odell Clarke, the Fenny Stratford brick maker, who had offices here.

Tiffany Close   Tiffany is a thin, silk-like gauze material out of which artificial Tiffany roses are made. The word is said to be a corruption of Theophany, meaning the revelation of God to man. The material was worn at Twelfth Night (Epiphany) celebrations and thus acquired its name.

Water Eaton Road   This is the old road from the village centre which connected Water Eaton to old Bletchley, and now leads to the centre of the modern town.

Waterhall Park   Running in a long, narrow strip between the Grand Union canal and the river Ouzel, this was the site of Water Hall, home of the de Grey family from *c.*1275 until about 1562, when the 14th Baron Arthur

Grey de Wilton decided to pull down the ancestral mansion and use the material to add a great hall, 50 feet long, onto his other home, Whaddon Hall. All the wagoners from miles around were summoned to carry the masonry of Water Hall to its new site, leaving only a large earthwork close to the river and a rectangular enclosure which were still visible in the 1960s, when all was levelled.

Willow Way   The willow family of trees contains many varieties ranging from small shrubs to large trees. The most commonly known are the osier, used in basket-making, the crack willow, which grows on river banks, the weeping willow with its drooping branches and the white willow, also known as the cricket bat willow.

THE LAKES ESTATE

Allen Close   Named after Lough Allen (Aillinne), which is in the north west of the Republic of Ireland, in County Sligo. The lough is at the foot of the Iron Mountains and the water drains into Sligo Bay (Cuan Shligigh).

Arrow Place   Angling and water sports are two of the attractions at the Arrow Valley Lake which gives Arrow Place its name. The lake covers 30 acres near Redditch in Worcestershire and a countryside and watersports centre was opened to all recently. The lake contains common and mirror carp, bream, roach, rudd, eels and perch.

Bala Way and Bala Close   Lynn Tegid, as Bala Lake is also known, is in Gwynedd on the eastern side of the Snowdonia National Park. The lake is 4½ miles long and a mile wide and is the largest natural lake in Wales.

Brora Close   Loch Brora is fed by at least five burns and the water from it flows into the North Sea near the coastal town of Brora in the Highland region of Scotland.

Burnmoor Close   Burnmoor Tarn is in the Cumbrian mountains and within 10 miles of the coast between Barrow-in-Furness and Whitehaven. The name is derived from the Old English for 'the moor of ancient remains'.

Buttermere Close and Buttermere Place   Named after a lake in Cumbria, whose name means 'the lake by dairy pastures' from the Old English *butere* (butter) and *mere* (lake). A mile and a quarter long and 500 yards wide, the lake is owned by the National Trust. The village of Buttermere is a popular tourist attraction.

Carron Court   Loch Carron is an inlet on the west coast of Highland Scotland, and there is a large reservoir in the Carron Valley.

Coniston Way   Meaning 'king's hamlet or manor', the derivation of the name Coniston is obscure. This part of the Lake District was a mining area in Norman times. It was on Lake Coniston that Donald Campbell died in *Bluebird* in 1967 while travelling at some 300 mph in a bid to improve on his world water speed record. There is a memorial to him on the village green.

Corin Close   No Corin lake has been found. It may be a mis-transcription for Lough Corib or Lough Conn in County Mayo.

Crummock Place   Named after Crummock (meaning 'crooked water'), a Cumbrian lake now owned by the National Trust. The lake is curved, which explains the name, and is 2½ miles long and a ½ mile wide. It is separated from Buttermere by a narrow strip of land.

Cullen Place   The only lakes found bearing this name are the Cullen chain in Minnesota, Canada. There is a village named Cullen on the Moray coast, Scotland but there is no evidence of a lake there. It is possible that an error may have occurred in the sign-writing, for there is a Lough Cullin which is part of the Lough Conn system of lakes, covering 12,000 acres in County Mayo, Ireland.

Dere Place   Dere Street is the name of a Roman road in North Yorkshire and Northumberland, but no lake of that name has been found. It may be a misprint of Lough Derg in the Republic of Ireland.

Diddington Close   Possibly refers to the small lake which existed at Diddington in Cambridgeshire, and was absorbed by the Grafham Water reservoir.

Doon Way   Loch Doon is on the north-eastern edge of the Galloway Forest Park, close to the A713 road which runs north-west to Ayr on the Forth of Clyde. In the Irish Republic, lough 'an Duin' is about 30 miles from the Atlantic coast of County Clare.

Dunvegan Close   On the Isle of Skye, the largest of the Inner Hebrides, the name Dunvegan is used on a loch, a head, a castle and a village.

Empingham Close   Named after a village in what used to be Rutland but became Leicestershire before being reinstated in 1997, Empingham (Anglo-Saxon for 'the estate of Empa's people') is less than a mile from the lake once called by that name but now known as Rutland Water. After 10 years' planning and implementation, it became an Anglian Water reservoir in 1976.

Ennell Grove   Fifty miles west of Dublin, Lough Ennell, or Loch Ainneann as it is known in Irish Gaelic, is one of a chain of lochs in an area of Westmeath, County Leinster.

Ennerdale Close   Situated on the western side of the Lake District, Ennerdale Water is actually a reservoir owned by the North West Water Authority. It is possible to walk round the lake, but there are few facilities for visitors.

Fern Grove   Lough Fern (Loch Fearna) is in the Irish county of Donegal, 12 miles west of the border with Northern Ireland at Derry.

Gairloch Avenue   A sea loch close to a village of the same name in the Highland region of north-west Scotland, Gairloch is a popular tourist destination offering safe, sandy beaches and watersports. An award-winning museum explains and interprets local culture and the Gaelic language.

Garrowmore Grove   This is possibly a lake in the vicinity of Garrow Tor on Bodmin Moor, Cornwall.

Garry Close   Presumably named after Glen Garry in the Perth and Kinross region, which forms part of the Tummel/Tay hydro-electric scheme; the loch is in the remote area of Craiganour and Atholl, surrounded by mountains topping 3,000 feet.

Gorman Place   Lough Gorman is a beautiful limestone lake near Ballintra, County Donegal.

Grasmere Way   The Cumbrian lake and village of Grasmere attract thousands of visitors annually. The lake, which is surrounded by fells, was a favourite of poet William Wordsworth, and the house in which he lived with his sister Dorothy is open to the public. The fields come down to the edge of the lake, providing the possible meaning of Grasmere, from the Old Norse for 'lake with a grassy shore'.

Gwynant Court   A lake in Wales, situated near the foot of Snowdon in the Snowdonia National Park, provides the name source.

Katrine Place   Loch Katrine in Stirling, Scotland forms part of some superb scenery, including woodland and moorland, and also supplies water to Glasgow. Just over eight miles long and a mile wide, the loch is associated with Sir Walter Scott's 'Lady of the Lake'.

Kinloch Place   Kinloch is Scottish Gaelic for 'lake end' and, with variations, is one of the most common names in Scotland, given to lakes, forests, a castle, a river and a number of villages, most of which are on the mainland, but there is also a Kinloch village on the Isle of Skye.

Laggan Court   A common name in its various forms and usages, Laggan is Norse for 'little hollow' and here it is likely to refer to Loch Laggan, which is on the edge of the Monadhliath Mountains in the Highland region of north-east Scotland.

Laidon Close   The shadow of the Grampian Mountains of Scotland, in a largely unpopulated area of the north-west region of Perth and Kinross, is the site of Loch Laidon.

Langdale Close   Great Langdale and Little Langdale are in the Lake District, separated by one of the region's smallest lakes, Elterwater. In Old Norse, Langdale means 'long valley'.

Leven Close   Loch Leven, in what is now the Perth and Kinross region of Scotland, provided a term of imprisonment on Castle Island for Mary Queen of Scots in 1568. There is now a hydro-electric power station at the head of the loch.

Lomond Drive   Named after the largest and many say the loveliest loch in Scotland. Loch Lomond is 23 miles long, up to five miles wide and 630 feet at its deepest. It is studded with 30 islands and is surrounded by hills to the south and mountains in the north.

Maree Close   A Highland loch close to the north-west coast of Scotland, Maree is 13 miles long and just under two miles wide.

Melfort Drive   Melfort Loch is situated near the Firth of Lorn on the west coast of Scotland in the historic county of Argyll.

Mentieth Close   The Lake of Mentieth is one of the many lochs and lakes in Stirlingshire, an historic county in central Scotland. The lake is small and contains three islands.

Meriland Court   No lake of this name has been found. Possibly Loch Merkland was intended, which is in the Highlands of Scotland, north-west of Loch Shin.

Ness Way   Sited at the north-east end of Glen More, Loch Ness is in the valley traversed by the Caledonian Canal from Inverness to Fort William. It is around 23 miles long and very deep, this fact resulting in numerous tales of a monstrous creature ('Nessie') said to live in the depths.

Nevis Grove   Probably named after Glen Nevis at the foot of Britain's highest mountain, Ben Nevis (4,406 feet). A river called the Water of Nevis flows into Loch Linnhe, close to Fort William in the Highland region of Scotland.

Rannoch Close   Named after a sizeable loch in Perth and Kinross, Scotland. Loch Rannoch is one mile wide and 8¾ miles long and drains into the river Tay.

Rimsdale Close   Loch Rimsdale is one of many lakes in a wild and remote area of the Scottish Highlands in what was formerly the historic county of Sutherland. It is fed by the Rimsdale Burn with water from the surrounding hills.

Ruthven Close   Named after Loch Ruthven, which is in the Highlands of north-east Scotland and some five miles from Loch Ness. It is one of several lochs in the area, fed by rivers and burns from the Monadhliath Mountains.

Rydal Way   Rydal is a small lake in Cumbria which receives water from Grasmere via a river which continues to Waterhead. It gets its name from Rydal village and is one of the smallest lakes, being three-quarters of a mile by a quarter of a mile.

Santen Grove   No lake of this name has been found. The nearest to it is Stanton Lake in the Wiltshire Cotswolds. Set in a country park designed and maintained by English Nature, the lake provides habitat for kingfishers and a variety of waterfowl.

Serpentine Court   Possibly named after the S-shaped body of water that was created in London's Hyde Park between 1730 and 1733, during the reign of George II. The lake is a popular feature of the park's 340 acres.

Sheelin Grove   Lake Sheelin (Lough Sileann) is in the Republic of Ireland at the conjunction of the counties of Cavan, Meath and Westmeath, some 40 miles from the east coast.

Skene Close   The Loch of Skene lies 10 miles west of the Scottish east coast port of Aberdeen.

Strangford Drive   An arm of the sea, 18 miles long and 6¼ miles wide at the entrance, Strangford Lough (Loch Cuan) is situated close to the east coast of Northern Ireland in County Down.

Tarbert Close   There are two lochs in Scotland named Tarbert. One, West Loch Tarbert, separates Knapdale and Kintyre, draining into the Sound of Jura on the west coast of Scotland; the other penetrates the island of Jura itself.

Thirlmere Avenue   Originally two lakes – Brackmere and Leatheswater – in an area which was bought in the late 1870s for the creation of a reservoir to supply water to Manchester. About 5½ miles long by half a mile, it is 160 feet at its deepest point, possibly providing the meaning of the name Thirlmere – 'the lake with a hollow'.

Torridon Court   In the remote Highlands of north-west Scotland, in an area which has been described as 'the wild outback of Britain', lies the loch which provides this name.

Tulla Court   On the western side of the Grampian Mountains in the Highlands of Scotland is Loch Tulla. The loch is fed by several rivers and burns, including the Water of Tulla, and itself feeds the river Orchy and Loch Awe as the water journeys south-west through Argyll.

Tummel Way   Tummel is a loch similar in size to Windermere and forms part of the Tummel/Tay hydro-electric scheme in an area designated a National Scenic Area in Perth and Kinross, Scotland. There are many fine walks around the loch and fishing is permitted from the banks.

Watten Court   This name is taken from the Norse word for lake or water, and here refers to the loch and village in the historic former county of Caithness, now part of the Highland Region in northern Scotland.

Windermere Drive   The longest road on the Lakes Estate is named after the biggest lake in England – 10½ miles long and a mile wide. The most commercialised of the lakes, the waters of Windermere attract visitors from worldwide to enjoy the boating, sailing and cruising – not to mention the scenery. The town of Windermere developed after the arrival of the railway in the 19th century. The name means 'lake of a man called Vinandr' and derives from an Old Scandinavian person's name and Old English *mere* (lake).

a

SELECT BIBLIOGRAPHY

AA Illustrated Guide to Britain, Drive Publications Ltd, 1971

Bentley, James, *A Calendar of Saints*, Little, Brown and Company, 1993

Chambers Biographical Dictionary

Grigg, A.E., *Town of Trains, Bletchley and the Oxbridge Line*, Barracuda Books Ltd, 1980

Macmillan Encyclopaedia, 1988

Markham, Sir Frank, *History of Milton Keynes and District*, White Crescent Press, 1973

Useful Websites

British Isles Top 100 Golf Courses: www.golfissimo.com

The Heritage Trail: www.theheritagetrail.co.uk

The Racecourse Association: www.britishracecourses.org

Illustration acknowledgements:

Bletchley Park Trust, page 20; Buckinghamshire Archives, pages 47, 68; Buckinghamshire Museum, pages 64, 67; Central Milton Keynes Library, pages 31, 66; *Milton Keynes Gazette*, pages 19, 43, 44, 70. Other photographs are by the author.